JOHN KINSELLA grew up in urban and rural areas of Western Australia. He is the author of thirty books of poetry, his volume *Peripheral Light* (2004) is edited by Harold Bloom for WW Norton. Kinsella is a Fellow of Churchill College, Cambridge University, and was formerly Professor of English at Kenyon College in the United States. He is a well-known poetry critic, having written for the *Observer* newspaper (UK) and *Scotland on Sunday*.

FAST, LOOSE BEGINNINGS

FAST, LOoSE BEGINNINGS

a memoir of intoxications

JOHN KINSELLA

MELBOURNE
UNIVERSITY
PRESS

MELBOURNE UNIVERSITY PRESS
An imprint of Melbourne University Publishing Limited
187 Grattan Street, Carlton, Victoria 3053, Australia
mup-info@unimelb.edu.au
www.mup.com.au

First published 2006
Text © John Kinsella 2006
Quoted poetry © individual authors
Design and typography © Melbourne University Publishing Ltd 2006

Edited by Sally Moss, Context Editorial
Designed by Nada Backovic Designs
Typeset in Sabon by TypeSkill
Printed in Australia by Griffin Press

National Library of Australia Cataloguing-in-Publication entry

Kinsella, John, 1963– .
 Fast, loose beginnings: a memoir of intoxications.

 ISBN 978 0 52285 254 7.
 ISBN 0 522 85254 8.

1. Kinsella, John, 1963– . 2. Poets, Australian—
Biography. I. Title.

A821.3

CONTENTS

To Tracy, as always . . .

Prologue: beginnings

I always find it difficult to begin at the beginning. I've got the kind of mind that jumps around, makes leaps to places it shouldn't, then twists back to the starting point again. When I am supposed to be working on something specific, that's the time I find best to be writing what I shouldn't. I think this is a common complaint or self-observation among poets. I like tangents. This is the third or fourth start to this book—a beginning is hard to find, maybe that's it. I think it's more to do with finding a starting point. I can make a statement like: poetry has been my life ... but what makes this so painfully true? Painfully. I guess it begins with my mother. Her pain. She grew up with a mother and grandmother Couper from the goldfields of Western Australia—Kookynie, out past Kalgoorlie. A ghost town now. My great-grandfather, foreman at the South Champion mine, died of miners' disease: dust on the lungs. I don't know about his poetry, but I do know my grandmother grew up listening to recitations of popular Scottish and English poetry, and that my mother's love of poetry came from there.

Well, that's not entirely true. My grandfather, Robert Sydney Heywood, who came to Australia from London with his mother, with sister Kate following a year later, brought with him a flair for drawing and painting. His father, my great-grandfather, had been an artist and, sadly, a wine taster, who died of an alcohol-related 'accident', while his mother had been a piano teacher. As we often heard, her sister, Aunt Minnie, sang at La Scala. Without tracing the mergings and tensions between music and art in my grandfather's life, suffice it to say that it was a battle for my grandfather and his mother to make ends meet in Perth, Western Australia, just before the First World War. My grandfather went on to do an apprenticeship as a sign-writer and to play the euphonium in the Perth Fire Brigade Marching Band. Apart from limericks, he did not have a big appetite for poetry, or literature in general—James Hadley Chase was his (very ironic) acme.

My grandmother, on the other hand, would recite Masefield and Tennyson and Burns and innumerable nursery rhymes. But from my mum's point of view I'm sure, the musical, the visual and the verbal were inseparable. Like the fairy tales my grandfather painted on my mother's bedroom walls—the stories that went with the pictures filled the room with music: threatening, inviting, whimsical and mysterious.

My mother started writing poems quite young. She stopped writing poems when I was about ten. I often talk about why my mother stopped writing when I discuss why I write poetry—her stopping, in many ways, is more important, to me at least, than her writing. As she would say: a lot of people write poetry. Giving up writing poetry didn't stop her reading it, maybe enjoying it even more. It's been a cornerstone of her life. It's been my entire life, and its beginning is her beginning. Before picking up on this thread, which takes me to my first meetings with 'professional' or 'published' poets, or whatever adjective best describes those for whom poetry is the cornerstone of life, I should mention my father's side of the equation.

That's the Irish side—the (ironically) true colonists of the immediate family outfit. The maternal Scots side which I mentioned above—the miners—came via New Zealand in the mid-nineteenth century and arrived in Western Australia via the Victorian goldfields in the 1890s. My father's mob came direct from Ireland to Western Australia in the 1850s. They were mountain people from County Wicklow, and my great-great-grandfather and his people before him were foresters—a rare thing in Ireland, especially at that time in the earlyish 1800s when only about one to three per cent of Ireland had any forest cover, due to the English extracting timber to feed their world-dominating navy.

These paternal forebears of mine left for the Swan River Colony (founded in 1829) in the 1850s, but instead of landing on the Swan River, or at the coast near Fremantle, they landed not far from Busselton, in the Vasse region, and quickly established a farm in tuart tree country. The process of dispossessing the Nyungar people of the area is not remembered in, or has been deleted from, family discussions and (the few) documents, but I have heard from the indigenous artist Julie Dowling that there's a Kinsella mob who are Nyungars. I have never met them, though I would very much like to do so. My inheritance is one of invasion and theft, and given the fact that this awareness and the desire for compensation to the victims and reconciliation (probably for myself as much as the dispossessed), is at the core of my own poetics, it strikes me that the Kinsella side of the family has as much to do with my poetry as the Heywood–Coupers.

The Kinsellas didn't actually stay long on the coast; they moved inland and after a couple of failed farms returned to forestry and, by the late part of the nineteenth century, group settlement. My great-grandfather Ned, charismatic and immense Irish-Australian standing nigh-on six foot four, like most of the males on the Kinsella side, was a group settlement leader who helped 'carve out'—read decimate—much of the karri forest region around Pemberton down to Walpole. He was 'successful' at his group settlement activities, even though most eventually faded and vanished. His son, Claude, went on to become a head state forester in the Jarrahdale region south of Perth, and, in fact, the entire Gleneagle area is still called Kinsella on forestry maps in his honour—a supreme act of renaming and deletion of indigenous identity.

Poetry didn't come through from Ireland in any shape or form for me. I once received a letter from the great Irish poet Thomas Kinsella to let me know he'd accidentally been sent a poem-proof of mine (from the *Times Literary Supplement*

[*TLS*]). In the letter he pointed out that we probably had common ancestry between us back no further than five generations. Clearly there was some familial poetic connection somewhere, but it didn't make its way to Australia. Or did it? As a child I read through my grandfather Claude Kinsella's forestry journals before destroying them through neglect, experiments and decoration—destruction tantamount to a crime. His spidery handwriting in indelible pencil, which ran purple blood over the graph-papered pages, seemed more poetic *and* scientific than anything I'd ever seen before. It struck me that to be a poet you had to be a scientist—or a forester—as well. It's the mix and match, the hybridising crossover philosophy that has led me to enjoy the poetry and company of voices as diverse as those of Australian poet Dorothy Hewett and the British poet JH Prynne, to enjoy the critical insights of Harold Bloom and Marjorie Perloff. The basic rule became: never be prescriptive.

Getting back to my mother. Throughout her difficult marriage—my parents separated when I was six and divorced when I was seven (one of the last cases, if not the last case, to be reported in the newspaper)—my mother wrote, against the wishes of my father, a practical man who was a motor mechanic by trade. That she won him a massive on-the-wall and fully decked-out tool chest by writing a poetic slogan did not impress him. Here is not the place to discuss it, but it suffices to point to the gender issues of the day, and my father's conservatism, as opposed to my mother's liberality. She published poems, stories and articles in a diverse range of journals and papers—from *New Idea* through to the *Catholic Weekly* (she had been a Methodist who converted to Anglicanism, though she considered herself open to most religions).

When she separated from my father, Mum went into advertising and specialised in copywriting jingles and snappy, catchall slogans. She earned enough money to head to university, during which time she made extra money by giving piano lessons. At university she was intensely involved with poetry on the level of study and as a writer. She published in *Black Swan*, an arts journal, and participated in the various poetic activities around campus. She entered the main competition for poets in Western Australia at that time—the Sir Thomas Wardle Bunbury Festival Prize—and came runner-up to Caroline Caddy one year, then won it the next. Her poems were getting known around the place, but then the divorce came through and she finished her degree and became a teacher.

Suddenly, Mum stopped writing poetry. Why, Mum? 'Because I got happy.' Mum only ever considered herself to be in the 'second rank' of poets in the State. As well as Wordsworth, Eliot, Keats and the other seminals of English-language poetry, locally she admired Dorothy Hewett, most certainly of the first rank, if a little eccentrically, who was also her teacher at university. Dorothy would tell me twenty or so years later that Mum was the best student of Wordsworth she'd ever taught. I recall Mum studying for her exam on holiday at Prevelly Park on the southern Western Australian coast. I heard most of *Paradise Lost* recited aloud, and grew bold with its awe.

So, beginnings are diverse and elusive. I suspect, however, that it was by the piano that the first poem came to me. By the piano, during the Meckering earthquake when Mum gripped my arm so hard, when the metronome made a new time, when the wires inside the piano spelt out words and the ground seemed ready to open up. I suspect too that this was a beginning of the end for Mum. Not sure why; instinct maybe. Dad was only vaguely around then. Separated, maybe. He wasn't long away from heading 'up north', to make a new start. Maybe he'd gone already. He'd been born literally in the bush. He was returning to the 'bush'—not a forested space, but a sparse and broad place. A place of mines. Of ongoing colonisations. Open on the piano, a first lesson book displaying a song whose words and rhythms have stayed with me as a poet: 'Swing low, Swing high, Swing me up to the sunny sky …' Like her then-recently deceased father-in-law Claude Kinsella's book-keeping in pencil, the letters jumped as the piano sang its weird previously unheard tune, graffiti-ing language in front of my eyes as the earth shook. It was a moment of synaesthesia. It has been present with me in all my interactions with poets—in that world, nothing says exactly what it seems to say. Anything is possible. And the proof of this claim follows …

To be a poet?

I spend a lot of time wondering what drives someone to 'be a poet'. There are many reasons one speaks or writes poetry—compulsion, catharsis, memory, therapy, the ineffable—but it's more perplexing that one should want to pursue it at the expense of all else, that it might not only give greater answers but serve as the template, even foundation, for a life. It's almost impossible to make a living from it, yet we attempt to do so. But maybe, for most 'life' poets, that's just a necessary side effect. Maybe there's a necessity that drives the 'art'. Ruth Finnegan, in her remarkable study *Oral Poetry*,[1] talks of the Eskimo shamanic poet Orpingalik and quotes a transliteration (into English) of his timeless 'My breath'. It is a poem about ageing focussed through the memory of male power and of providing for wife/family/community through hunting polar bears and seals on the ice—now he sings, 'Sick I have lain since autumn, / Helpless I lay, as were I / My own child', asking of his wife 'how long must she go a-begging'; we hear of loss through age and sickness. The poem, however, works as renewal through absorbing his pain.

Of the polar bear:

Let me recall the great white
Polar bear,
High up its back body,
Snout in the snow, it came!
He really believed
He alone was male
And ran towards me.
Unaya—unaya.[2]

1 *Ruth Finnegan*, Oral Poetry, *Cambridge University Press, 1977*.
2 *ibid., p. 181.*

The explorer Rasmussen, who went through the 'Eskimo lands' of northern Canada in the 1920s, transcribed Orpingalik, explaining his songs thus: 'Songs are thoughts, sung out with the breath when people are moved by great forces and ordinary speech no longer suffices.'[3] The idea that the song is as essential as breath, and driven by breath, is common to Orpingalik and to many, if not all, of the poets and critics of poetry (who are also poets) that I've met. Even the most ironic and self-conscious poets are singers and articulators of this breath; they write out of necessity. And yet, all live in conflict with this compulsion, all work against the feeling of futility.

A critic like Harold Bloom lifts the 'great' work into a canonical Pantheon, and for him the necessity of reading and of being shown a truth, or sharing an insight through the genius of the poet, is what makes life worth living. His elevation of the text, of the thing in itself, of art for art's sake, is often at odds with the difficulties of living the life of a poet. The romance of the occupation, and the hardships it brings, drives the machine of poetry. Resentment comes when the poet scores a tenured university position or is heavily funded by government or private organisations—the artistry is seen as suffering through the comfort, predictability, security. But most widely known poets have some trick to making their lives work, to greater and lesser degrees. Women poets of nineteenth-century Australia published as intently as their male counterparts, and yet, critical and academic apparatuses being what they are, they are

3 *ibid., p. 183.*

forgotten or are belatedly resurrected. Privilege of memory makes for longevity as much as 'talent'.

Tom is an old friend from school days who was always going to make it as a poet. He says that he is okay if alone, because he lives in the cave in his head. I kind of guessed this at school—and also, living in my own cave in the head, I respected the sanctity of his. I've never been so content living in mine though—I think when I started drinking seriously at fifteen and sixteen, it was in an effort both to break out of my cave and to pull down the rocks overhanging the entry. I destroyed myself with alcohol and, not much later, drugs, because I could not resolve this paradox. My interest in poetry, and in those who write poetry, has been driven by this ... contradiction.

Recounting the lives of poets as I have experienced them—sometimes over long periods of time, sometimes briefly—has made me reflect a lot on the nature and necessity of poetry. I stand condemned myself for revealing things as I think I've seen them: I just know that, for all my escapades, knowing poets has mattered much to me.

1

On not finding Kansas—yet

DOROTHY HEWETT. Who, in her autobiography *Wild Card*, remembered events with a filmic sweep. Who co-opted stories and tales into her own stories and tales. Larger than life, a blonde Cathy coming out of *Wuthering Heights* at an obscure angle. Of the wheatbelt, of South Perth and the River, of the Communist Party, of her own sense of romance. Dorothy, Dorothy, Dorothy. We all loved her. I loved her. *If I were younger*, she said, but it was *not* being younger that made me love her. It was because she'd *been* younger, and that this youthfulness constantly fought through age and ailments. They invented the expression 'young at heart' for you. So, you liked 'bad boys'?

I have written many (many) poems for Dorothy and I still have the outline of the book we were going to do on relationships, but abandoned. 'I'll only do the book if we can tell the bad relationships as well.' There were legal repercussions; she had been censored. Maybe she said things she shouldn't have—made claims. But that's part of it. I am on the grounds of the University of Western Australia as I write, and place is so important to memory. It's a trigger, but also the place of stories particular to memory.

I remember Mum came home when I was a kid and said: 'My tutor, Dorothy Hewett the poet, is having an affair with the gardener who is just outside her window during tutes.' *Wuthering Heights*. Merv, her husband, as Heathcliff. Bizarre. I sometimes wonder if my memory of her is a series of anecdotes and *bons mots* pasted together by obsession. What was it we saw in each other? A knowledge of the wheatbelt—of the parrots, the sheep, the heritage of racism and violence? The colour of wheat fields before harvest? And the smell. Yes, that. But the dark side of things—the side people condemned—her children, her sex, her runnings-away. For me, the drugs and alcohol and extreme behaviour. People don't like obsession. But she did. At the Western Australian Premier's Literary Awards one year when I didn't go, my partner Tracy told me Dorothy arrived in glorious gold lamé sweeping to the ground. 'Why isn't he here?' she asked. 'He has a problem,' Tracy replied. 'The smack …' she said, knowingly, loudly, in front of everyone. 'I like the bad boys.' Dorothy hid pity and sorrow and understanding all in one.

When I was about eight or nine, Mum said: 'My teacher is having a few of us around this evening to talk poetry.' The next day she told me of the girl playing the violin, how all the kids ran around the house half-dressed or undressed, but free. It was told by way of contrast, but sympathetically. She described the little girl intensely. And the squawking of the violin. That girl was Kate Lilley, Dorothy Hewett's daughter, who would go on to be a unique poet in her own right.

I became fascinated by Dorothy Hewett, this teacher of Mum's. I heard some of her poems, but can't recall how. They reminded me of 'The Lady of Shalott'—Tennyson was often recited at home. She reminded me of something out of the Wizard of Oz—somewhere between Dorothy and the Wicked Witch of the West. I have a vivid picture of her tangential beauty. I imagine I saw Dorothy on one of my many visits to university with Mum. I think she spoke to me, but I only remember the images, and hearing her poems in another voice elsewhere.

I fall off the Greyhound bus from Perth. I am wired on a mixture of wine, amphetamines and downers. I've been awake for days and am near the end of wakefulness. The crash is hard then. I have come in search of the poet Robert Adamson, who tells me we're on our way to meet Dylan and Knopfler at their Sydney hotel, pre-concert. It's February 19th, 1986 (the most tumultuous year of my life), and I've been twenty-three for ten days. Bob Adamson is in a borrowed V8 Commodore. We drink at a pub in the Rocks and it gets out of hand. His Dylan obsession was made clear to me the first time we met. Dylan is a prophet, he's William Blake, Bob would shriek. He played the records over and over. We drive to Sydney's Darlinghurst to pick up Dorothy. I have a vague memory of being invited into her bedroom and wondering why. She'd be about sixty-three and is talking about her lovers. Another male is in the room but he leaves. She is brushing incredibly long golden hair— it had to be golden. I start off sitting on the edge of the bed but, feeling uncomfortable, take a seat near a window. We talk about my problems with drugs, and whether or not making love is better; I go for the drugs. I have a full-time girlfriend in Perth but we've broken off. Before her I'd been with her sister and this remained an issue. Another former girlfriend was a prostitute. This fascinates Dorothy. Bob bursts in, crazed and jealous, his hair jolting with static. He is raggedly dressed and keeps saying wildly 'Fuck, man' and 'Dylan is fucking great. He's seen the abyss, he knows the beast.' He looks at Dorothy and starts screaming at me that I am a traitor and of the beast. And so begins a long pattern that will define Bob's and my up-and-down rela-tionship. Dorothy thought I was dangerous; and back then, I probably was. I was a polyglot drug user with paranoia and obsessive-compulsiveness thrown in. I mixed with a genuinely violent bunch of people, who made good their threats. Small wonder I would eventually become a pacifist.

Then we were in the car. Someone whose memory is no doubt more vivid than mine and can contradict at leisure was in the front next to Robert. I was in the back seat with Dorothy. There might have been another person. But I was next to Dorothy with my head in her lap and she was stroking my hair. Things were spinning. I was tripping out. Maybe tripping literally. Robert was agitated. We're seeing the fucking greatest, and you guys don't seem to care. He was at Dorothy as much as me. The other/s in the car remained silent. Robert drove around the main streets of Sydney into darkness, slowly, but with angry bursts. I don't know if we saw Dylan and Knopfler—I passed out, and when I came to, we were parked in Darlinghurst and no one else was in the car. It was early morning and I let myself out of the car and started walking towards the Greyhound bus station, a good way off. I wanted out; though it was only a few months later that I was back again.

Flashback to July 2nd, 1983 … when I met Dorothy at the same time I substantially and disturbingly found Robert Adamson, angel of the abyss. I remember exactly when, because I saw Verdi's *Il Trovatore* at the Opera House and it began another of my obsessions. Joan Sutherland in the lead, with the Sidney Nolan backdrops which have made a lasting impression on me … the orchestra was conducted by Bonynge, and a professor of architecture invited me home in his Porsche. I declined.

That afternoon before the concert, I watched small boys hauling ships into the bay. It became a poem in *The Frozen Sea*, which came out a few months later. I tracked Robert down in Balmain—at the Balmain hotel where I think he read that night, or, if he didn't, was meeting with other poets. Maybe Nigel Roberts. Always sarcastic, Nigel. I drank a lot and we argued—all of us.

Mid-1984 I went in search of Robert again. He'd read and liked *The Frozen Sea* and had invited me back. Robert took me for a drive in his expensive car—a gold BMW he'd bought with the money he and Dorothy had got as an advance on a film script ... or Dorothy had gone guarantor ... or both—and we visited the publisher Hale and Iremonger, over something to do with the last, never-published issue of *New Poetry*. He told me I was a visionary, and I didn't believe him but wanted to. Things got really bad on that visit and Robert thought I was sleeping with his wife, Debra. (The story goes that Debra, after first having slept with Robert, said: 'I've just fucked Australia's most famous poet', and a wit responded: 'Who, Les Murray?') He physically fought with Debra and swilled bottles of whiskey and drove over the Sydney Harbour Bridge, doing a ton, looking for cigarettes. I left on that occasion with Bob's enmity and an inscribed copy of his book of poems *The Law of Heart's Desire*.

The Ghost of John Forbes[4]

It rained for 24 hours
when Forbes died
the loose iron flapped
in the summer storm

4 *from* Halfway Up the Mountain, *Fremantle Arts Centre Press, 2001, pp. 138–9.*

why are they dying
these young men in their middle age
leaving the landscape diminished
the poetry poorer
Martin Johnson   inheritor
of a tragic history
What day is it? they asked him
Bloomsday he said & died
of alcoholism
on a straightened bed in Casualty
Robert Harris with a dicky heart
found God and died alone
in a rented room
now Forbes had gone
that footloose bumbling creature
writing his stylish witty poems
hooked on cough mixture
leader of the poetry wars
in two cities
and the young men
the elect   the chosen
who are no longer young
the savage critics
the middle-aged statesmen
of letters   grow grey   close ranks
mourn in their suburbs as I do
it's Australia Day   the traffic

mounts up on the hard-driving highway
what ghosts out there
who won't come home tonight?

Dorothy Hewett

When Dorothy wrote this poem she was not well her-self, though she would live another four or so years. When she died, I couldn't stop writing poems for her—in them she became a water bird, 'maybe a white-faced heron' (known locally as a 'crane') or, even more likely, an egret. I was convinced because when I heard that she'd died, a pair of egrets moved into the flooded gums down the back of our place in York—we were back from Ohio for a few months. We'd spoken to Dorothy on the phone from America when we heard she'd been diagnosed with cancer and hospitalised for what most imagined would be her last illness. On the phone she seemed overjoyed to hear from us—'So good to hear from you darl … are you behaving?' I don't think I've cried since I was a very young child, but I almost did then. For both Tracy and me, she always seemed part of us. And I think we were part of her, in the way that all younger poets (and maybe older ones as well) were. She took the community of poetry seriously.

Her comment in the above poem on the death of Australian poet John Forbes—that he was the leader of poetry wars in two cities—is made somewhat equivocally. There's a mild touch of irony, but she saw the necessity of resisting the status quo, of 'fighting' for a new poetry. Indeed, she liked the frisson of action—after all, her class battles and her Communist-Party politics had been essentially resistances to the middle-class values from which she knew she couldn't separate herself. Dorothy did not have the romantic attachment or feelings towards John Forbes that she had so strongly toward Robert Adamson—the 'bumbling' is an (uncharacteristically) anti-romantic observation on Dorothy's part. There was respect (maybe as she would for any cadre if she were fired up for the cause) on an intellectual level, but not on the physical level. For it to be the whole deal, you had to feel as if Dorothy wanted you sexually, and that only 'age' was a preventative (the romance being that it shouldn't be, that 'age' is a construct that society forces upon us). The prospective Harold and Maude, if not actual. Dorothy's heart was well and truly Merv Lilley's, but there were always rumours of affairs on both sides. People (archly) marvelled at what drew them together and kept it all in place. Public as Dorothy was, that was where the 'no one's business' sign went up. One could observe that Merv devoted much of his time to being Dorothy's secretary, carer and attendee (in a positive sense), and that Dorothy well knew it. Merv had to find time for Merv.

Dorothy went searching for what I later went looking for myself: action and a passion for poetry above all else. I grew more bitter, addicted, and aggressive towards the world at large; Dorothy constructed a role for herself, a cocoon of myth, in the same way as she imagines she did as a child (Alice), or maybe as Tammy Wynette did in styling herself as the First Lady of Country Music.

It was often said that Dorothy 'held court'—that, having been delivered by Merv in their massive black hearse-like American car, Dorothy would be seated (on velvet, if possible), and that all would gather about her, to praise, to listen, to be heard. She enjoyed it, but she also had a sceptic's eye and was self-critical enough to know the way leeches worked. She and her audience fed on each other. Varuna in Katoomba, New South Wales, a writers' centre and the former home of novelist Eleanor Dark, was where she held sway in the last decade of her life—she was First Lady of the Blue Mountains literary community. People forget, because in her ballet slippers she was spotlit in the auras she gave off, that being so overweight and unwell bound her to the chair. She held sway because she couldn't comfortably move far. Merv's immense strength ('a barrel of a man', I've heard it said many a time) was always there to ensure her security. Merv, photographer (buying second-hand lenses, cameras, and bits and pieces of photographic equipment), writer, labourer, is one of the sharpest men I've ever met. He mocks quietly, and would never hesitate to say what he thinks. He plays the class origins to allow him to enter the middle-class soirées and cultures to achieve this. In his book *Gatton Man*, he implies his father was a murderer and he fosters a benign intimidation that could be much more.

Three occasions

Three occasions with Dorothy stand out in my mind now. The first was the dinner held in her honour after the launch

of *Wild Card* at the University of Western Australia. The
second is the book signing and then conversations in her
hotel room (and a radio interview) during the 2000
Adelaide Writers' Festival; and the third, which runs the
risk of rolling a couple of separate visits into one (one with
Tracy, the other alone), was time spent with her at the Dark
Cottage in Faulconbridge, the Blue Mountains.

The first, after the *Wild Card* launch, was an Anthony
Lawrence co-conspiracy that went wrong. By that stage
Anthony (poet and friend) and I had begun to fall out and
the evening was punctuated by his needling me and drunk-
enly rivalling my drunken behaviour. Dorothy sat amused
(though it was her occasion) as Anthony and I traumatised
the other guests with extreme stories. The dinner took
place at a Subiaco restaurant. I didn't eat at all, just drank
as much free alcohol as I could. I never asked who footed
the bill, or maybe I threw fifty dollars in at the end and
didn't think about it. Dorothy was dressed glamorously.
Merv was assisting her with most of the mobility issues.
The flight from Sydney had been horrendous for Dorothy
and she wasn't really very well. The launch itself, by the
then-Premier of Western Australia, Dr Carmen Lawrence,
had gone well. There had been hundreds of people in a
hall-like room, and Dorothy had read superbly from the
'autobiography'. As soon as I heard the first few lines of
text, I knew liberties would surely have been taken with
memory. Tracy and I often think, as we drive past the
Midland railyards coming down from York, that the
romance of the working class (from a young communist

woman's point of view, especially one who'd grown up on a sizeable rural property, then lived in South Perth by the river, her grandparents owning a local cinema), while brilliant and even noble, is wide of the brutal reality of making a living and the dirty politics of the shop floor (especially then). That's what Dot could do: she could mythologise, maybe even 'elevate' to song, the harshest reality and make it a paean and a ballad of darkness melded with hope. There was something 'anonymous' and universal and primal about her singing. As time went on, though, irony changed the nature of these paeans, and a great darkness hung over her work.

I don't really remember who was at the post-launch dinner other than Bill Grono (also drinking heavily, and immensely funny, Bill had edited Dorothy's *Collected Poems* and was a lifelong friend and defender of her work and legacy, a bit like the Home Office of Dot in WA); Bruce Bennett, still then editor of *Westerly* and a long-time Hewett supporter, critic, and fan; Anthony and myself; Dot and Merv; and Carmen Lawrence. Anarchist that I was—and those were my pre-pacifist days, so I was a highly volatile and aggressive activist (frequently being arrested)—I really hit it off with Carmen. Anthony seemed annoyed—we'd been at each other's throats all evening. Dorothy watched Anthony and me intently, and she seemed to enjoy her young male admirers fighting in front of her. Carmen started drinking with me. I downed a glass; she downed a glass. I couldn't believe it. I told a dirty joke; she told a better one. I talked about anarchism, and she discussed the interest she'd had in anarchism in her student days at the University of Western Australia. She was smart—I mean really smart. She spoke of the opportunism and ruthlessness of party politics and how it made you, in many ways, what you weren't, and that to stay true to your beliefs and pragmatically put things into effect was the greatest challenge. She told me about her guitar-playing son. I, enemy of all government, had found a mate who was a state premier (and she remains a friend).

The evening began its natural decay, and Dorothy whispered to Merv, and then Merv told the guests, that Dorothy had to return to the hotel. Her legs and feet were swollen from flying, and moving, and she was feeling ill. We all kissed her and gave appropriate praise, and she was gone. Anthony was well and truly pissed-off with me, so he got up and said, 'Well, I'm going. You coming?' I said no, and he wandered off.

Carmen's driver poked his head into the restaurant looking for the Premier, and with that sublime skill she has of keeping the eye of the person she is speaking to, and catching the eye of another without making you feel you are being looked over, she let him know she was on her way out. I think she might have covered my drinking bill (out of her own dough, not the State's, more's the pity!). She was so immaculately attired, even her glasses had remained straight and not a hair out of place while she was drinking and carousing. Total control. I think that's what makes Carmen far more radical and downright clever than people might even realise—she toes the line, keeps steady on her feet, but remains her own person. I'll escort you out, I said. Unkempt and dishevelled, drunk and high, I escorted her on my arm out to her waiting car. No, no, let's walk a block, she said, and sent the car down the street. Arm in arm, and somewhat leaning on each other for support, we went off down the road with me reciting Keats's 'Ode to a Nightingale', which I can still do off the top of my head (I once memorised the first sixty pages of *Finnegans Wake* as the ultimate party trick). And there her driver was, door open for Carmen, and into the car she went, and off to her other life. Or maybe she'd never left that other life. When she finished being premier, I tried to convince her to take a position in Cambridge: she's one of those people with whom you could discuss issues day in, day out. I think my motives were selfish. This is not to paint a picture of a saint; as she'd be the first to admit, politics is a messy and disgusting business, and one betrays one's views no matter what they are the moment one plays the game. But she's a genuine lover of the arts—and an anarchist, if only at heart!

A digression

I'll get to the other two occasions shortly. But thinking again over Dorothy's poem for the ghost of Forbes, the lines

> Robert Harris with a dicky heart
> found God and died alone
> in a rented room

remind me of Robert Harris, who John Forbes thought had the greatest of poetry minds. They were close friends, Forbes and Harris, and Forbes wanted me to see Harris's greatness. When I met Robert Harris, he'd just stopped working in a sex shop because his skin had started to rot, and he blamed it on God punishing him for his sins in working there.

I was supposed to be at Harris's place at around midday but didn't get there until the evening because I fell asleep in Martin Place. I'd been in the Cross speeding the night before, and had ended up drinking from sun-up. I caught the train to Martin Place, thinking I'd get a taxi from there, but curled up on a seat and fell asleep. I'd been awake for days. By the time I got to Harris's place, Forbes was ropeable. You bastard, we've been waiting. The translation of this reads: 'I am hanging for a drink and you've got money and I want thee (my interpolation: it was a little like that … and he did like the metaphysicals a lot …) to buy a bottle of whiskey or vodka or whatever.' I told him I'd fallen asleep in Martin Place and he forgave me (after getting fifty off me on 'loan' for a bottle and Camels): 'Beautiful John, that fucks up Australian poetry … Martin Place deserves it.' Robert Harris was keen to talk poetry, and after I recited Forbes's 'Stalin's Holidays' off the top of my head (with a few errors which Harris corrected— Forbes had gone to buy booze), we set to discussing 'Jane, Interlinear', the masterpiece (as Forbes had described it) that Harris had been working on and that I would soon publish in its entirety in the journal I founded, *Salt*.

What was remarkable about Harris was his 'giving-ness', a generosity of spirit that Forbes clearly revelled in and was proud of. Harris had wit like Forbes, but not in the same razorish way. They wouldn't have got on if that'd been the case. Harris was more visionary, a more Blakean figure fucked up by paranoia and religious detritus. He admired the clinician and sceptic in Forbes: it seemed better self-preservation. I am not sure if it was the one room of Dorothy's poem, but I only recall a room where we sat around a table jammed tight against the wall. It was very close, very humid with breath, smoke and drink. I left late and went back to the Cross. I can't recall a single thing about Harris's appearance, other than thickish white hands. I don't really know if they were his or Forbes's grabbing a glass of spirits. I think they were Harris's hands …

Subplot: it's war!

The identity of Australian poetry of the last four decades has bogged down in the idea of 'poetry wars'. In recent years the dynamic, that generational urge to change what's come before, has shifted, but from the late 60s it dominated poetry publishing, reading and criticism. The story has been widely told elsewhere, but in a nutshell, it finds its origins in the Robert Adamson-inspired takeover of the Poetry Society in the late 1960s, and the imagined rivalry between *New Poetry* (magazine) and *Poetry Australia*. In the same way that the United States has had its New Formalist reaction to 'Language poetry', so Australia had its new poetry reaction to the traditions of rhyme and meter and conceptual conservatism that defined much of Australian verse at the time. The qualification of these differences was expressed in rival anthologies: John Tranter's *The New Australian Poetry*, for example, versus the anthologising of Robert Gray and Geoffrey Lehmann. The aesthetic and political differences between the camps even became polarised around individuals: Les Murray versus John Tranter, or Robert Adamson versus Robert Gray.

So much of it was a boys-versus-boys construct. If John Forbes was perceived as a leader, it was because the more conservative camp/s feared his polemics, his wit, his intelligence. John had the human touch and could take most people on in their own terms. In some ways, I think he engendered trepidation because he himself was far more conservative than many would have allowed. John Tranter was also a figurehead, but he had an aesthetic edge that removed the battle from the grime of the street. Forbes was more threatening, because he had that element of the 'brawl' about him, and his faults, 'bumbling', were more on display. There seemed a willingness to get dirty.

In the early 90s (and onwards), I was being critically identified as belonging to the Forbes camp—not only through our friendship but stylistically (which I found bizarre). In reality, it was a funding issue; Forbes supported my funding applications, and later was a panel member of a board that gave me money. This created outcry that made it into the papers, and Robert Gray and others (underestimate them at your peril) inspired articles in the *Sydney Morning Herald* analysing what kind of poets got what. The factional wars came down to funding. I never saw myself as belonging to anything very much (what club would have me?) and I wrote an article for the ABR, *Pulped Factions*, that said as much. But in the late 90s, the internet had created new networks of 'mates', critics attacked the demarcations and even argued that 'lines of gossamer' linked poets and so on. It had all become touchy–feely, and then tokenistic and representational. Truth is, the camps argument was always a Sydney–Melbourne white male thing, and those who made more than that of it had vested interests in doing so. Dorothy never really belonged herself, though her sympathies lay with Forbes and co.

... the second occasion

The second occasion I mentioned earlier was the Adelaide Festival in 2000. Over the previous year or two Dorothy and I had worked on *Wheatlands*, our collaborative book of writings on the wheatbelt, displaced by generations. I was living outside Australia by then, and Dorothy had written much of her wheatbelt poetry at a distance, physically and spiritually: 'mourn in their suburbs as I do ...' My poetry, on the surface, seems more bitter than Dot's, but there's a darkness lurking in even the earliest of her wheatbelt verse. I felt we were in dialogue, and that nostalgia had no part to play in it, despite Dorothy calling her ten years of childhood on the farm in the Great Southern: 'a treasure house of poetry for me'. She also says in her introductory prose piece to *Wheatlands*:

The eyes of the adult and the eyes of the child see differently. The glass darkens, there are only hints and flashes of that lost world. The bush, its birds decimated, falls ominously silent, erosion carves up the land and the white patches of salt deaden the paddocks. Yet something durable remains; a sense of space.[5]

There was a massive crowd at the Adelaide *Wheatlands* reading. Dorothy, sitting, began by reading some of her poems from the collection and talking about her childhood growing up near Wickepin. I then read a batch—'The Silo', 'Goading Storms …' and others—and talked a little about my uncle's farm Wheatlands, my times there, managing it while my uncle and auntie were overseas, living with my shearer brother, and so on. It was conversation more than a reading. We were both excited. One of my favourite poems of Dorothy's, 'Legend of the Green Country', though set in an earlier generation, could only have been woven out of the same kind of stories I grew up hearing. The problems of creating legend out of what amounts to dispossession concerned Dorothy increasingly as she aged, but those problems were always there. Speaking in the 'lingo', she ironised her own position as teller of the family's tales, as well as participating in them:

My father was a black-browed man who rode like an Abo.
The neighbours gossiped, 'A touch of the tarbrush there.'

5 *Dorothy Hewett and John Kinsella*, Wheatlands, *Fremantle Arts Centre Press, 2000, p. 9.*

The consciousness and the pride in association with Aboriginality (despite the derogatory 'Abo': a term offensive to indigenous people now, as then—there's an irony regarding the use of language, and towards the inherent racism of the community) was always there. It showed especially in the sometimes scathing depictions of racism in Dorothy's plays. This consciousness of the wrongs done to those whose land was stolen and the desire to rectify them were a major bond between us. At that event, as I was speaking about land rights and the necessity for returning land, I noticed a middle-aged bloke with a land rights beanie pacing up and down at the back (distant back, outside the tent). I am not sure who his people were—he didn't say—but he spoke of 'our people' being all indigenous Australians. He stopped, looked up and yelled: 'You go on about giving land back, but what are you doing?!' I told him about how both Dorothy and I had requested that all profits from *Wheatlands* go to a local wheatbelt land council (a request we passed on to the publishers, and hoped was met—we didn't receive royalties so I assume some kind of arrangement was made). I shouldn't have said it, because largesse is a guilt reaction. As an old Nyungar bloke (and others) said to me once: 'Guilt won't bring our land back.' I've heard that said many times by many people since. And it's true.

After the reading we went to the book tent, signed maybe two hundred books (people tripped over themselves to speak to Dorothy, which she handled with generosity and enthusiasm, calling them 'darl' and other pet names). The crowd was mainly late-middle-aged women, with the odd young bloke sparked up by my anarchism and Dorothy's ex-communism. Confusion there. I wanted to speak to the guy who'd yelled out. I couldn't see him. I wanted to explain the poems: how they were laments rather than celebrations, how even when an idyll was conveyed it was always bittersweet. Always irony. After that day, I became more determined in my campaigning. It's the only answer. As Midnight Oil said (before Garrett went G-Man): 'Give it back ...'

Dorothy was exhausted and returned to the Hilton, where we'd all been put up. I went to her room later, and talked with her daughter Kate and Kate's partner Melissa. I'd been reading Kate's poetry since she won the 'Shell' poetry prize back in the 70s as a thirteen year old. She had a notorious reputation when I was a teenager: hanging out with older poets, writing verse that was ten years more sophisticated then her age allowed, acting a small part in *The Chant of Jimmie Blacksmith*.

A friend at the University of WA said to me the other day that a family member (of Dorothy's) had told him that Dorothy and her sister had basically spent their lives 'doing whatever they wanted'. It seemed true. I convinced Kate that she should publish a manuscript of poetry with *Salt*. She did, and the book, *Versary*, would become one of our best titles. I hadn't seen any of Kate's poems in print since an issue of *Southerly*, and before that in the *Penguin Book of Modern Australian Verse*.

I think Dorothy had learnt as much as she needed to know (or cope with) about paranoia through her life and activities in the Party, through surviving relationships privately and as a writer, trying to make a living, and through her ex-husband Les Flood's chronic paranoia. I believed Dorothy in most things, even when she embellished the truth for the sake of a story. As Tracy says, there's a scene in *Wild Card* where it seems she has adopted and adapted part of the plot of a German girls'-school story as a kind of (unconscious? or conscious?) template to relate the events of her own life. (The film was *Mädchen in Uniform*, based on the book *Das Kind Manuela*.) Dorothy was always the fusing of art and imagination, at least to me. That evening, as the sun lowered through the tinged window, Dorothy and I recorded our thoughts and memories for an Australian Broadcasting Corporation (ABC) radio programme.

... and the third occasion

Dorothy's enjoyment of youth was a defining factor in her writing. It made ageing all the more profound. When Tracy and I visited her together in Faulconbridge, in the Dark Cottage, we arrived on the train from Katoomba and were picked up by Merv in the great car, to be taken to Dorothy. We stood in the kitchen chatting with Merv, before he went straight to mopping the dirty dishes. The kitchen's a mess, he said, more by way of recognition of a certainty than an exception. Somebody usually came in to help out, I seem to recall, but hadn't arrived yet. There was a chicken carcass on the table and there were books lying around.

We were taken into a lounge-sized room, but still low and claustrophobic (which I like), ceiling-to-floor with books. Peter Minter is going to sort them out, Merv said. He's going to be Dorothy's secretary. As is Merv's way, he gave a cheeky look (only way to describe it: as a younger man it was probably a very different look), and said: 'That'll give me some writing time.' His jokes about being Dorothy's secretary were always double-edged. I doubt he could truly countenance anyone else being that close to Dorothy—for to be close to Dorothy is to be close to her work—but he did genuinely crave the time for his own writing. He intimated that, as Dorothy was the main breadwinner, he had a responsibility to look after her needs. It was more psychological than that, like the dark front-room library of the Dark Cottage.

When I visited Dorothy on my own a couple of years later—2001, maybe 2002, picked up by Merv again as I came up from Central to Faulconbridge Station, winding up through the Blue Mountains as if it were what all wheatbelt poets might do if choosing to live elsewhere in Australia, the contrast so strong as to make it compulsory—I was taken to the new back working space where Dorothy was seated, and she spoke about her interest in Tracy, her interest in her work, her interest in how we fitted together: once again, the couple in writing. After patiently saying that he'd leave us to talk over work (we were planning a new book on relationships), Merv began to laugh and said: 'I am laughing at you because we call you John Satori at home. You know, satori.' He walked off slowly, still laughing.

2

Big Les

Disclaimer

LES MURRAY AND I have more than the rural in common. We have a history of depression—though mine tended to pass when I managed to get 'straight'; that is, to kick drugs and alcohol—and inner torments (I still have them). We also have a defining history of being bullied at school. The origins of Les's 'black dog' have been traced and discussed by both Les and his critics, and most accept the bullying as a major part of it. With a public figure, the statement of fact is always going to be dismantled by claims to the contrary.

Some say that Les's being bullied at school either led to, or should be reconsidered in the light of, his purportedly being a literary bully now. What does this mean? Something along the lines of his way being the right way. Mainly that, rather than directly accuse or abuse someone who displeases him, he uses literary 'henchmen' to do his dirty work. I've been on the filthy end of things regarding these supposed henchmen, but I can honestly say that I am sure they've always operated alone and without encouragement. Their dislike of me needs no prompting or motivation from Les!

Personally, and certainly on the surface, I have always got on well with Les. Maybe the problem is that I've always got on well with a couple of his major 'enemies' too. John Tranter and Les Murray are so often set up as diametric opposites, and they certainly have a history of having a go at each other: the rural nationalist in Les, the urban modernist in Tranter. The arguments are slightly more sophisticated than this, but that's where the origins are. Truth is, Tranter is every bit as rural as Murray, and even went to an agricultural school. He sees no nostalgia in his rural background.

Les has a way of saying things in the bravado of the moment, that are actually cryptic connections with the sufferings and problems of others. He often sounds racist talking of indigenous Australians, but I believe he actually has a deep caring and affinity for Aboriginal peoples everywhere, especially those of Australia. What might seem appropriative in the 'Buladelah–Taree Holiday Song Cycle' is actually a deep plea for connection, not overlay. Les is a whole lot more complex than many would like to think. So often you hear: great poet, awful person. He's the same as poet and person: even the most obvious lines in his work are difficult, and his most obvious social interactions are the same.

There is a little story that takes us slightly off course. To be interested, and to think you are being respectful of cultural difference, is not necessarily to be so, of course. Les has angered many indigenous Australians by talking of them in paternalistic ways and by simplifying complex argument. His doing a draft of the preamble to the Australian Constitution at Prime Minister John Howard's behest did nothing to increase possible understanding.

Recently, at the Sydney Writers' Festival, I was talking with Les about my commitment to land rights. Blinking and looking away, occasionally taking sips of his drink with a finger cocked, he said that he looked forward to the time of land rights for whites as well. He was serious. He said that whites would not be able to abuse the land, and that it would be passed down to offspring with the same laws governing it. As always with Les's reasoning, you can see the kernel of respect for the land in there, and, by creating a positive comparison, for indigenous law and belonging as well. But the end result of it is to displace the indigenous. At best, this is how Les is so easily misunderstood; at worst it's what it seems.

As the beginnings are hard to isolate, so are the middles and other points on the timeline. I flash back from Sydney, but forward from the wheatbelt of Western Australia. Cambridge—we'll be there a little more expansively shortly.

Medieval university town, where history aches to prove that modernity owes all to it—good and bad, it feels it can take it all. Where only dons may walk on the grass; where dons don't talk to each other walking the streets lest they destroy an incipient great thought. Where self-satisfaction vies with scholarly dedication. For Les, his intellectual crisis of academia versus free thinking is confronted starkly there. He seems to like being in Cambridge, but also seems to like observing its follies. He has said to me that he has some interest in the poetry chair at Oxford but is generally suspicious of all universities, even though he'd admit they have helped 'make him'.

At a Cambridge University English Department function, I introduced Les to two colleagues. Firstly, to Ato Quayson—an Africanist from Nigeria. Les asked him where he was from and then commented on his blackness. This was no discussion of Césairean negritude, but of what a black man was doing in Cambridge. Ato admired his bluntness, I think, and answered directly.

The second person I introduced him to (though I've heard him speak of this since, rearranging the details of meeting) was Germaine Greer, who was keen to meet her somewhat notorious (though in a different way from her good self) fellow Sydney University student. Germaine Greer has an imperious way of greeting anyone—I recall how, when she met Tracy for the first time, she stood in her flowing silver dress with silver pixie boots (Tracy says: 'I don't recall her wearing this. I thought she wore a slaty blue dress, and certainly not boots …'), looked Tracy up and down, then turned away to continue her conversation with me. What this does for the sisterhood, I'm not entirely sure. What was fascinating about Les meeting Germaine was that two people you would normally expect to be at each other's throats engaged in polite and respectful conversation. Les seemed the kid in the interaction, and Germaine the schoolteacher, but it went like clockwork. So it cuts both directions in the public respect stakes, I guess. Never trust random observations, though. Forget about the pronouncements and what you see out and about. Biography lies. Witnesses aren't always witnesses.

So, the major thing we have in common is having been bullied at school. Admittedly, severe bullying does make you a bit of a Jekyll and Hyde character. No matter how much you try to balance it out over life, deep hurt remains. It defines you. I can't speak for Les, but I can speak for my own experiences, which were deeply traumatic.

The bullying I underwent was serious physical hurt— smashed nose, lips, skull, and numerous other injuries that required medical attention. It was systematic and remorseless. Let's just say I wasn't called 'Dictionary' out of respect for my vocab. I set myself up as an outsider intellectually, and was treated as such. Who I was annoyed people, and who I am now probably still does the same. My defining characteristic then and now is enthusiasm. And that's a hated trait. It will get you called 'crawler' or 'suck hole', even when you're the one standing against everything authority represents; when you're the one who refuses to do sport, to work in a particular environment, or who protests to the point of being locked up. It's hardly worth validating it all. The end results are indisputable, though.

Les saw all this in me the first time we really chatted. He said: 'You have a lot of issues.' And I told him about plenty. We met in the Castle Hotel in the main street of York. He was there for a conference where he was guest of honour. I had arrived early that morning from the city where I'd been visiting my then-partner—we had begun an intermittent separation during which I spent most of my week down at Williams with my shearer brother, Stephen. Stephen would go to work early and I'd spend the day drinking, staggering through Dryandra forest, and attempting to write poems. Poet and academic Dennis Haskell had invited me to drop in on the conference to meet Les. I was chatting to Dennis about this just recently, and he said I poked my head into a talk and briefly said hello to Les before meeting him later that morning in the bar. Apparently, the professor running the conference was alarmed and annoyed by the presence of someone as clearly 'out of it' and bedraggled as I was.

After finishing the conference session, Les went to his room. I had been drinking for a while when he came down the stairs of the Castle. The bar was busy—it must have been a weekend. People pushed against us—a few were shearers I recognised through my brother: tough and potentially very violent. Les seemed unperturbed; in fact, he seemed quite at home in such company. No veneer of middle-class famous-poet respectability. It was telling. You have to know that scene well, which I did, to know when someone is genuinely comfortable. I've seen Les far more uncomfortable in the middle-class milieux of Sydney and Cambridge.

I drove Les out to the family farm. I was somewhat pissed and agitated. I told him of my decaying relationship with my partner—a long-term partner with whom I had a son—and of my traumas in the drug world. It's little surprise he has since resorted to talking of me in cryptic anecdotes. Les has a wry sense of humour as well. Funny thing is, everyone I'd known—his closest friends included—had always made jokes about his weight, as Les in his poems frequently does himself; but, to be honest, I barely noticed the Robert Morley body and only heard the Robert Morley wit, plus a good dose of humility and caring. People often talk of Les's size—and he has been extremely and unhealthily rotund. He works the image as a kind of defensiveness, and though his bulk fits with a nationalistic poetics of sprawl, it's not, to my mind, who he is. After his illness that almost claimed his life some years back, the illness that he says (I don't believe it) ended his 'black dog', he lost an immense amount of weight. Why are people so concerned with Les's looks? It is worth checking out his eyes some time; they retreat deep into his head but look far off into the distance.

I told him of my hell-life at school and we silently concurred. It was one of those moments that, no matter what happens between us—at least on my side—will remain as a connection. There's a kind of rapture when someone understands such declarations so deeply. I can't understate what an influence Les's work had on me as a teenager—he seemed to make the world possible through the Australian landscape I knew so well.

What Les had that I didn't have, and never will have, is the certainty of religious belief. I have faith, and I believe in redemption, but I am opposed to all organised religion. This is the gap between a convert and one who has left a church (Anglican in my case). It's the tangent that takes me into a disruption of language that Les will approach purely through irony or even disdain. The Language poets remain babble to him, though he believes he can write 'innovative' poetry as well as they do. The Language poets were (and still are, to some extent) a loosely affiliated group of American poets (or 'practitioners') who started publishing in the 1970s in self-edited small magazines. They felt that the alienation brought about by modernity was not captured in the lyrical poetry of the day. Avant-gardists, they were interested in the politics of making the poem and the politics made by the poem. For me, this sort of linguistically disruptive verse is about disrupted belief, whereas Les needed more than the healing of poetry to hold his bullied and disappointed world together.

The drive to the farm takes you along the Goldfields Road—the old track to Kalgoorlie, long bypassed by the distant Great Eastern Highway, but still a road along which you'll find Hunt's Well and cross the Meckering faultline—and then off onto the gravel of Mackie Road. The road then was thickly treed with wandoos and, further along, with sammies, or salmon gums. Les commented on the unusual trees—so familiar to me. Turning into the farm gate with its cattle grid and wagon-wheel greeting, he couldn't but notice the vast spread of salt on the land beyond: your muse, he said. The muse of destruction and loss and complex and addictive beauty. He insisted we later go down to look at it.

When we reached the farmhouse, my Auntie Lorraine celebrated his arrival—she deeply admires his poetry—with tea and scones and even a rendition, with her singing partners, of a celebratory song. Les was touched. Big Les, as they call him, was humble and polite. It was part of my Auntie's social fabric to feed people upon arrival. My grandmother Heywood, she of the litany of memorised poems, greatly liked Les. She was only a few years from her death then, and she treasured meeting him. I was feeling pretty ill but the conversation kept me hooked.

Les's many years in the city had altered his sense of country but not vanquished it. We walked down to the salt, and he and my uncle named the many trees planted in an effort to reclaim saline land. My strongest memory is of Les switching flies on his back with a looping arc of the arm as he walked and talked. I chatted with him about the salt and the remarkable reclamation project that had begun twenty-five years earlier. It is said that it was the first consistent and persistent programme of its kind undertaken privately in Australia. The salt would become pivotal to all our lives in a variety of ways.

Hazlitt's essay on Coleridge and Wordsworth resonates here. Just before I started to write this book the British poet

Jeremy Prynne asked me to read it and I did so, closely. In the way that Coleridge composed while walking rough ground, and Wordsworth smooth, I now see that Les made of the rough the smooth, and that movement itself works hand in hand with conversation (as it did for Coleridge especially). He was thinking poems, as was I, as he walked along the reclaimed fringes of salt lands.

Cambridge

It was a few years before I again saw Les in person. The next time was in Cambridge where I was living with my wife, Tracy, and daughter, Katherine. In some ways this is my partner Tracy's story as well, as she and Les really hit it off over the short time of their meeting—sharing Catholicism and an interest in foreign languages. Tracy had once joined and left the Carmelite order (as well as the Church) and this disturbed and interested Les.

Les visited us a couple of times in Cambridge when we were there and once or twice when we were away. The first time, he came to town for the Cambridge Conference of Contemporary Poetry (CCCP) and stayed in Guest Room 1 in the College. He did a couple of readings on that visit, including one in town attended by Tracy and the Master of Churchill, Sir John Boyd. Les liked that when we told him.

In the same way that the University of Western Australia, or the farm near York, or Sydney, or later Kenyon College would be, Cambridge—the place itself—was inseparable from people for me, probably more so than anywhere.

It's the island where people come to you, that you don't have to leave to see people, unless you want to. Erasmus hated it—so cold and damp—but still, Erasmus to Cambridge came! The CCCP forms a branching away from the main body—to some, a virus—in the rounds of poetry in Cambridge. It is an experimental poetry conference; there were many who found it hard to understand that Les was invited. Though the reading went smoothly and was well received, it was one of those rare moments in Cambridge where the 'mainstream' got inside the avant-garde. Rod Mengham, who helped with the invitation, rightfully saw that innovation has many faces, and that what Les does with the vernacular, and linguistically, is experimental in its own terms. His attendance was a watershed, in my opinion. Anyway, again, I digress.

The morning after Les's reading at the CCCP, I met him in the Copper Kettle café where he was breakfasting. He was irritated by the conference payment he was to receive, which was 250 pounds if I remember. He wanted a larger payment—and probably fair enough. This would create much upset in the committee, though in the end it was sorted out. What fascinates me about the occasion was the manner in which it was broached, indirectly, through his speaking to me in the café. Les was working on a new manuscript—or, rather, was about to deliver one to his British publisher, Carcanet, and was leafing through the poems. I asked to read some, and he allowed me to do so. I discussed my alternative view of his poetry—that it can be read as a reflection on the instability of language rather than the certainty of world events and the materiality of history. He thought it viable. Leaning back in his chair, with his glasses up on the top of his head, he tilted so that the glasses began to drop. He trained them into place, studied a poem, picked up a pencil and wrote the name of a journal next to it. *Rialto* have taken five of my poems, he said. He was, as he often does, wearing a pullover that didn't quite fit. I can't recall the colour. He picked at some food—a bit of egg had stuck to the wool, worked its way into the stitches. 'My daughter loves music, though I am tone deaf,' he said. I'd hear him repeat this on a Desert Island Discs session on the BBC in 2000. It was said like a mantra. I thought how musical were the poems he showed me. Some argue Les is not a musical poet, but then they try to impose a metrics on the verse that never existed for or about it in the first place. You need to listen differently to his poetry. Then he mentioned his autistic son and told me how he turned on everything on the stove. And then he mentioned that he suspected he himself was slightly autistic. There was a build-up here—intensely personal information that had found its public sound bite but was painful nonetheless. Then he said he relied on readings and writing for income—it was his only way of making a living. He asked for the money from the CCCP. I agreed, and got it dealt with.

The poet John Forbes (who said he didn't care about poetry as a career yet obsessed over it more than any other I'd met; who said he could *make or break* a career; who worried about his posthumous reception; who was a triumph of contradiction) once said to me that his greatest achievement for me—and he did greatly help me poetically (to understand my own verse and many poetic failings)— was to ask and get a blurb from Les Murray for the back of my poetry book *The Silo*. John used to remind me of this regularly.

People always placed Murray and Forbes in opposite camps, but Catholicism lapsed or dismissed goes deep; they were Catholics together, albeit in different ways. Forbes greatly admired Les's verse and liked Les, with all his 'wrong beliefs', a good deal. When John went begging for money, Les helped out. The influence each had on the other is one of the strongly neglected areas of Australian poetic cross-pollination.

As John Tranter has said to me of Les's disturbing poem 'SMLE' about a gun—his celebration of the Lee-Enfield rifle—it's a celebration of a weapon and that's that. Tranter noted in an interview I conducted with him recently,

And I remember the scorn in my father's voice when he mentioned that a certain farmer owned and used a .303 Lee-Enfield, the standard British military rifle for over sixty years. More than five million of them were made, and they were sold cheaply as army surplus after the Second World War. The Lee-Enfield provides excessive force for any purpose you might have in mind in the bush around there, and they had a lethal range of two or three miles, which was very dangerous. Only an idiot or someone from the city would use a thing like that. We hated the city people who occasionally came into the bush to go shooting. They would leave gates open and shoot at anything that moved.

When I read Les Murray's poem about the Lee-Enfield—a kind of paean to the military virtues and their symbols—I thought he was crazy. Country people don't talk like that.

What Tranter says is true, though I remember as a kid using any weapon I could get hold of, for the sheer adrenaline and testosterone rush. Forbes was also obsessed with military hardware and was nationalistic, as is Les. Start looking, critics; start looking!

Ohio

Kenyon College is a liberal arts college in Ohio which sits in a sea of deep Grand Old Party conservatism. The corn and soy fields are surrounded by woods, and in normally flat central Ohio the hills of this area hide things away. It's a hunting zone, with deer and raccoons and anything else that can legally be stalked and shot with gun or bow. It's not unusual to hear rifle shots in the vicinity and to see magnificent stags dragging from the backs of pickups, their antlers not far from the bitumen. With the peaked hats and camouflage come the visits to the village by Amish people, who live in large communities a short way north, centred in the town of Berlin.

In their horse-drawn black buggies, dressed in heavy black cloth, hatted and bonneted, they sell basket-ware and wood-work to visitors. They are renowned for craft, for removal from modern ways, for the intensity of their faith. They live lives that are parallel to those evangelical Christians who are replacing evolution in schools with so-called intelligent design. In this place so familiar with a broader patriotic conservatism—nearby Mount Vernon proudly calls itself the most Republican town in America, its Civil War munitions-profit houses going hand in hand with its place in the history of the Underground Railroad, a strange relationship epito-mising the contradictions that make up central Ohio—newer 'radical' and intensely localised religious conservatisms have sprouted from the roots they set long back.

In 2001 I received an e-mail message from Les's editor at Farrar, Straus and Giroux, New York. By that stage I had been installed as the visiting Thomas Chair at Kenyon, where I would later become Professor of English. The FSG editor wanted to paste together five or so readings for Les in the United States for his new selected poems there, *Learning Human*. The title encapsulates Les's world view— the alienation of the bullied self from the social world, a socialised humanity. In religion, he finds equality and an absolute; among people he is misunderstood and isolated. He reads to large groups of people to feel part of a crowd that he doesn't want to be part of. He craves what repels him. He can't be liked in the way he wants to be liked. There are issues of sexuality here, suppressed, we imagine, by bullying. The sub-human redneck has a language he wants the listener to respect, to learn, as he learns their manners and their ways. Les has always been a traveller, and, coming home from the cities of the world, is conscious of detachment from his place. In the migrant ethnicities of Australian identity, he belongs and recollects and connects with the migrant past, despite resisting 'multiculturalism'. He can't go back but keeps testing the waters.

Les's reading at Kenyon was a major success. He read in his familiar way—knowing his audience, crossing cultural boundaries with finesse in his understated roughness. That's his stage under-presence. When he has finished he smiles at the applause and pauses for it to continue. He and I walked and talked. He was curious about my position, wondered if it would suit him—there was much talk of getting him there as a visitor. The academic side of things bothered him, though he was assured of his creative freedom. And being away from home for so long. Family. Also Bunyah. But the money appealed.

I am reminded of walking with Les down Middle Path— so named because it suggests the middle way in life (neither too much nor too little) but also because it connects the two ends of the college. Traditionally, the path meandered between the old dorms and the faculty of theology—fitting for a college founded by an episcopal bishop with an unusual name, Philander Chase. Chase was the first bishop of Ohio, and his vision of education is not so distant from the values that still underlie the college. He had his own house built within sight of the college, with a window looking out towards the college chapel.

On this occasion, it was a chilly though not *very* cold day, though Les and I had been reading of a cold snap somewhere. Les said, in that way he has of being decisive yet leaving it to the air so that any challenge might be directed diffidently: 'So much for global warming.' One always has the feeling Les is playing a persona, a mask, when he makes such comments, as if he's expected to say it. I've no doubt Les has a more sophisticated understanding of global warming issues than this, and in many ways it was probably said to test me, but it was characteristic. In fact, it brings to mind another example from one of his stays at Churchill College, Cambridge.

I met Les early in the morning after he'd had his breakfast in hall, at the Churchill Senior Combination Room. I had it in mind to ask him a few questions about that poem of his that has long angered, delighted and generally obsessed me—the 'Buladelah–Taree Holiday Song Cycle'. We arrived at the same time and glanced at the newspapers, laid out near the coffee machine for the edification and enlightenment of the Fellows, and both caught the headlines. It was the morning after the massacre at Port Arthur, Tasmania's notorious old convict prison turned popular tourist site. We both expressed shock, horror and disgust, and read as we stood. The poem was forgotten. In the disturbed quiet that followed, as other Fellows moved in and out of the SCR, Les said: 'They'll blame guns—but it's not guns, but people, who kill people.' True, but there's an expectation that someone from the country will say this. The implicit defence of the right to bear arms is there— even though I might add that Les had pointed out how context and restriction of types of firearms differentiates Australia from, say, America regarding gun control. Even so, it was clearly a major issue for him. For me, as a pacifist, there are no reasons for guns to exist—this is anathema to Les, and maybe a cultural contradiction.

An aside. When I interviewed Les for *Meanjin* in Sydney a few years ago, I met Robert Adamson and his wife Juno Gemes in the same hotel lobby where I had conducted the interview earlier that day. Robert was so pissed off about my having spent that much time with Les that he leapt onto a table and started screaming *traitorous beast abyss* stuff. 'None of you see it, none of you see it, I ...' People had gathered for an evening drink and the more they began staring at him, the louder he yelled. The gist was that poetry is above all politics, is above everything, and that Bob had dedicated his life to this Mallarmé-inspired conception of 'purity', mystery, celestial-ness, to the ideal ... and that all others were pretenders. Juno calmed him down. She's great at that. Bob needs her—and, she would agree, she needs Bob.

Afterthought

I've never met Les's wife Valerie, but have spoken for a few seconds with her on the phone. She seemed stalwart and a believer. I don't know anything about her relationship with Les, but people speak of her with respect. Poets are difficult to live with, I know that! And Les won't be any different. I did meet his daughter in Cambridge and, though shy, she grew excited talking about music. Tracy and I once drove to Bunyah to see if we could find Les, but we couldn't. We did look over the district though, and it helped place his poems. There's not only a *sense* of place, but there really *is* place in the work. These are very different things. He observes up close, in his own way—he sees and misses as anyone being *of* something does. It's easier coming from outside sometimes. Maybe his long residence in Sydney helped him see again, as do his travels away to the cities of the world. From Bunyah, we headed towards the Great Dividing Range and, crossing it, saw some of what Les sees; maybe other things he hasn't seen, or wouldn't want to.

3

Pas de deux

LOVE AND WAR? At school, C. called me 'Dictionary', like the others, and a teacher lover, a 'crawler', because I liked teachers more than kids, and he hated me and even pushed me against the lockers. He was a 'big boy'—in Year 10 he bullied me hard, in Year 11 he talked quietly to me on a few occasions, in Year 12 he knew I *knew* and would say nothing ... He wanted me to be his partner, and for four years I was, in a sense, I guess—just a friend. But not as he wanted, and it frustrated him.

It was the first night we were away on our grand trip from Bali to Britain. (In the end, we only made it to Nepal, where we were involved in a serious mountain bus crash, C. suffering injury, and we were eventually flown back to Australia on insurance.) That first night he lay naked on the bed on his open sleeping bag, Bali so hot (even up in the mountains around Ubud) and the monkeys still chattering from the monkey forest and the garams' cloves thick in the air with Indonesian beer and the ganja we'd found—he asked me if I would, and I said: I don't know, I just don't know; it feels all wrong. And he would say this was the culmination of years of teasing, and I would say: I don't know, I don't know.

Then, when the bombs had gone off in the Hindu holy city of Varanasi, India, and people had been shot in the streets below our balcony, and dysentery had left us stranded, I said: Now it doesn't seem to matter, but C. groaned and turned back into the darkness he'd started to inhabit. I was reading Lenin—a cheap edition printed in Moscow in ten volumes we'd bought from the same stall where an elderly guy deftly rolled Bidi cigarettes full of tobacco and un-named herbs while-you-wait, and made food offerings to peripatetic cows out of a bucket placed a short way out into the street, and C. read and re-read a copy of *Lord Jim* we'd picked up in Calcutta before our escape from the dealer who held a gun at my head and demanded I smuggle narcotics for him. C. sat on the end of the bed as the explosions went off, rocking back and forth, calling his bed the Patna and insisting he was Lord Jim. Overwhelmed by cultural difference, but desperately trying to find an 'in' without the spirituality that would have helped, I could only quote Lenin on revolution. I still can't make sense of it, of the senses that had overworked or failed or led to that, regardless. The guy who looked after our room locked the large, wooden, double front doors of the hotel and rushed to our room, telling us to stay put—It's an inter-family battle over alcohol, he said, but we knew it was something more than this, and looking from our window at old Lee-Enfield rifles aimed across the rubble, we talked about our time sitting by the Ganges near the ghats where the cremations unfurled and a holy man offered to take us down one of the sacred lanes, or to a holy place of learning with its stone pool and green waters, filling our emptiness with Lord Kashi Vishwanath, with one of the twelve Jyotirlingams of Lord Shiva. Even through our haze, we registered the holiness of the place, and its commercialism, and the waiting for death as bypass … the city promoting itself as 'the city of death and liberation', sacred, most holy place of knowledge.

After school C. and I had little to do with each other for a while, though he found me towards the end of my first year at university, staying at my grandparents' hundreds of miles south, in the city. The Big Smoke. Perth. Within a few months I would move out, and basically vanish. But then it was still Victoria Park by the railway line where I wanted the girl of my own age—who smoked at the station every morning before catching the same train, who looked rough, who looked from a world of sex and drink—to notice me. She did, I know, looking back, and I spoke to her once and she reacted, but I took it no further. I worried about my thoughts being overheard. So C. came around then, and drove the two of us through the hills up to Mundaring Weir, in the family Mini Moke, at dangerous speeds. We were both adrenaline junkies, as they say. Risk was good.

He looked big, too big for the Mini Moke, which made it crazy, outlandish. It was a blast to be out there, berserk through the hills. His zone, his old stomping ground, before Geraldton, before his family broke up and the boys went north with their father, who showed me my first 'fuck film' on a big screen, a huge television with three coloured beams that he'd hire out to pubs, making his fortune. C.'s father was a schemer, a dreamer, an entrepreneur. C. wanted to be like him, in part, and was *municipal*. It was perverse, I said, him being a junior town councillor, a lover of the law, of the Church, of being a prefect and of authority in the school. He loved power, and he loved defiling power. See him heavy, hanging out of his jeans, shirt fluttering and mousy blond hair ruffled—tangling—in the wind as the Moke, close to the ground, made its own air-effects, pulled itself down into potholes. Exhilarating, ridiculous. Drowned in his late twenties, he is buried there now, where we drove. I have never seen his grave.

What did he think: a single line in *Uncle Vanya* was an acting career? The Perth stage a hotbed? I would write plays and he'd act in them. A kind of fantasy, at eighteen. What did he think as the villain in the school melodrama? Year 12. We crossed paths backstage. I was a cabbage-headed headmaster opposite the Head Girl. It was *my* lead and I remembered all the lines. It seemed a wordy play, and the play for me was words. The play for C. was action melodrama ... directed by my mother: capes, moustaches, sweeping across the stage and doing the evil thing. The laugh, the look. His eyes the dominant thing. Really, letting it flood over me: overwhelming, but the eyes. Sometimes limpid brown, but sometimes almost green and electric, always when trying to possess, to burn the other soul. My mother was disturbed by C. but liked him and liked his love of theatre.

We read *Cities of the Red Night* together. Our reading defined our actions. We saw the film *Naked Lunch*. Words hurt, irony some comfort. At a party, talking about Warhol's autobiography as we ran out back and over the fence, the cops blooming like pop art. In my Chairman Mao cap and with the silver cigarette-box C. had given me filled with Chesterfields, I was an anomaly of his and my creation. He was jealous of poets and artists and musicians, and wanted me to himself. He said that to live was to rot. I agreed.

4

Fellow travellers

THE SAIL AND ANCHOR was, and no doubt still is, Fremantle's most popular pub. I'd spent a lot of time being thrown out of it, and even begging in front of its doors with a similarly dreadlocked friend of mine (Cathy) for enough money to buy a bottle of sherry, before being removed by the bouncers. Actually, the bouncers there weren't so bad—in the Metropolis nightclub next door they were horrors, and one beat me so hard in the alleyway alongside that I collapsed in a heap in the middle of the street. That was for smoking pot just outside the side exit. I heard eventually that a bouncer around the corner in the Federal Hotel beat to death a friend of mine, Dave Trotsky (who wouldn't let us drive home without turning every corner left—difficult). I lived with Cathy in a run-down duplex in Martha Street that amounted to a squat with a ten-dollar-a-week rent attached to it, and the walk to the Sail and Anchor was not a long one. But Anthony Lawrence was to come after those days.

I first met Anthony in 1989 or early 1990, after he tracked down my mother's place, where I had been staying on and off during difficult times in my then relationship. He asked to have a drink at the Sail and Anchor pub and it sounded okay to me—drinking was good.

What enticed me and amused me about Anthony was he seemed to think he was Dylan Thomas. He loved the idea of being a poet in a way that was alien to me. I had met poets through my mum as a child, I'd corresponded with a few, I'd had wild times with Bob Adamson and the Sydney poets, but I had compartmentalised them as being away from my regular life which was about drugs, alcohol, and activism … and trying to keep a relationship going, the best way I could.

Here was someone who loved poetry as much as I did, but apparently without the bitterness (later on, I had a different impression altogether on this), without an anger towards language (which he has never discovered, as far as I can see). He drank heavily and was on hyper-drive. He seemed to have whatever mental and emotional problems I had, and maybe even a few more. I could tell he spun lies, but that was okay as well. Just like any other drinker, but with a verbal facility second to none, and an amazing ear. We recited poems and got drunk, and that set a pattern for the surface; beneath, a rivalry and enmity formed the engine.

I wanted to go on to drink at the Stoned Crow, but Anthony had to go somewhere, he said. I went on and later that evening he turned up with a girl who seemed stunned and bemused. She hung on him as he dribbled poetry, and then they disappeared out to his Land Rover. I never saw her again. She was a one-day stand—didn't even make it through the night. Might not seem much of my business, but it was part of that engine that kept the flywheel spinning at high speed.

I had less contact with Anthony when he was living in Carnarvon, but an intensity returned when he moved further south to Geraldton. I had spent the last three years of high school at Geraldton Senior High School and knew the town well. I've always thought of Geraldton as a nexus or nodal point, a place where very different cultures meet, overlap, clash, and layer themselves. It has its problems. It is a racist place, although I use the word carefully but with relevance. The divisions into difference are masked by the touristy 'seaside' demeanour of the place, which is in fact misleading. The former premier of Western Australia, Geoff Gallop, comes from Geraldton, and when I was talking with him at an awards dinner a couple of years ago, he made an astute observation: 'Many in Geraldton spend too much time talking about Aborigines'—meaning that they obsess over Aboriginal people not out of respect, as they should, but by way of racist dialogue and ranting. If the divisions are between fishermen, farmers, townies and country people (though Geraldton sells itself as a country town that's becoming a city in the mid-west), they connect in their bigotry towards indigeneity. There is a strong Yamatji presence in Geraldton and a strong sense of Yamatji community. When I was at school, there were racial fist fights on Front Beach down from the Leisure Centre pinball parlour every Friday and Saturday night.

There are numerous examples in Geraldton of police brutality towards indigenous people, and the general racist malaise of Australian society is writ large there. Carnarvon, where Anthony Lawrence had been, and where my father lived for many years, is even worse, if that's possible. Many called it one of the most racist towns in Australia. It's where the belligerent federal MP Wilson Tuckey rose to power—called 'Iron Bar' Tuckey, so it is said, because he attacked a 'drunken Aborigine' with a metal cable one night in his pub. The cable is mounted over the bar there. As a teenager, I think I saw it—I was certainly taken to his pub.

But back to Geraldton … It seems strange to begin a description of a place by a comment on its racism, but for me as a teenager there, that's what defined it. All I seemed to hear was race hatred, to the point where a school friend I fell out with told me of his dad stockpiling weapons to use against 'the blacks'. Also hated by the white majority were Asians (as they were described), and 'wops'. A Greek–Australian friend of mine at school constantly copped it for being 'greasy' and so on. This was commonplace and part of the Australian experience. In Geraldton, it was magnified. Isolated, many kids at school had never travelled the five or six hours to the city of Perth in the south. But Geraldton was large enough to be self-contained, to cultivate its resentments. The town extended into the Chapman Valley, the Chapman River being quite polluted. The ranges behind it marked the semi-arid zone, with agriculture extending down a relatively narrow strip along the coast. The main feature of the town was the port, where ships loaded grain and mineral sands. During high school, I worked holidays and weekends at a laboratory that served the mineral sands industry, and also helped supervise the loading of ships with monazite, rutile and zircon (taking intermittent samples for testing). The American military would arrive, and I was shown a nuclear warhead locked (then unlocked by drunken officers) in the bowels of a missile carrier. People have told me it couldn't have been, but I am sure it was. I've been reading Thomas Pynchon's technical reports for the Minuteman missile project. Truth is scarier than fiction.

The massive wheat bins were and are the main feature of the place—beacons for the town. There's also a cray factory over that way—crayfish being the sacrificial lambs of the sea. And Point Moore lighthouse, with its candy-red stripes phallically impaled before the surfing breaks of Hell's Gates, Neons and Explosives. The high school is a short distance across an oval from the town shopping precinct, right next to the sea and railway line (just recently rerouted in a classic destruction of an entire ecosystem of dunes surrounding the town). I was beaten up numerous times crossing that oval, adjacent to the Anglican cathedral (where a friend had been molested years before as a thirteen-year-old altar boy), walking towards the Catholic cathedral, a Hawes building written about by Philip Salom in his first volume of poetry, *The Silent Piano*.

Across from the Catholic cathedral in Geraldton are the town library and shire offices. And now there's a large theatre. Beyond those buildings, Norfolk pines planted fifty years before—down Durlacher Street. My old headmaster planted some as a kid, if I recall. Geraldton was deeply conservative, and at school there was a re-enactment of (governor–explorer) Gray's expeditions into that region. Little sensitivity to indigenous concerns was shown. That was for WAY '79, a celebration of 150 years of 'settlement'—or colonial occupation, as I'd prefer to say.

I am not sure how much of this Anthony registered while there—he certainly registered the sea, and car parks, and places for eating, meeting, having sex, fishing.

Anthony was attracted to these towns by the coast and the fishing. (He and I were dramatically on opposite sides of the equation when it came to fishing. It's one of the big things he has in common with Robert Adamson, and a prime bond between them.) But in terms of where he went to live, he was primarily following his wife, who worked there.

Where does one begin with this? The book that came out of Anthony's time in Carnarvon and Geraldton was *Three Days Out of Tidal Town*, published by Hale and Iremonger as part of their Australian poets series. Anthony's constant shift between publishers had already generated tension by this, his second full-length book. Ocean, blood, sperm and alcohol were the generative fluids that drove this work (and others). It includes his masterpiece, 'Blood Oath', and an amalgamation of bits and pieces from that period. Sequences and single poems work in tension, making it a slightly bitsy book. It includes his notorious 'The Fire Danger Board', actually written about a visit to poet Rod Moran in Yanchep, Anthony watching the Fire Danger Board being changed due to hot dry weather and then deliberately changing it back to a low setting. There's a pathology in this that runs through all Lawrence's work. The criminal in dispute with the romantic, the question becoming, Is there any difference?

Even his sensual poems are elemental, and *Three Days* is a typically elemental book. The coast represents escape (out to sea), and a numinous and liminal area for him—a sufferer of anxiety attacks and a variety of phobias, by his own admission. Forbidden sexuality and its zones—beaches, car parks—are the undertones I associate with Anthony's conversation about these places. I remember him telling me about being in Carnarvon with a bunch of young trawler fishermen as they sat watching porn on a video and masturbating, to see how far they could ejaculate. Whether this is true or merely fanciful anecdote, it says something about the hunting/fishing–sexual metaphor that haunts his work.

The first time I visited Anthony in Geraldton was comparatively controlled; the second time was entirely out of control. The house the Lawrences had scored was just down from St George's beach, right at the front of town. You crossed a road and there was the sea. A few weeks before my then partner and I arrived from Perth for a visit, an object had been thrown at the house (I can't recall what), and Anthony had become agitated. I think he assumed it was a cuckolded partner. Almost fifteen years later and I am still running into his alleged 'ex-es' or admirers. A couple of years ago I was interviewed by a journalist in Geraldton and asked whether I knew Anthony. The poet. She rolled her eyes and made a strange, throaty, *grrr*ing sound, then shook her head. 'I knew the poet. A lot of women here knew the poet.' She shuffled on her chair and I asked what she wanted to talk about. The poet?

With a bed on the floor of the lounge, my partner and I settled in for the weekend. We got changed, and Anthony managed to find his way into the room. Okay. We went down to the beach for a swim. Only Anthony and I went out. Anthony keeps lunging under the water and circling me. I am drunk and do my usual tread-water-and-drink-from-a-stubby trick. Anthony emerges. I thought so, he said. He'd been looking up my cut-off-jeans trouser leg. A year before we'd been at the Irish Club, drinking and listening to some kind of performance. Anthony asked how 'liberated' I was, while telling me that he wasn't homosexual. We then shared a French kiss in front of the conservative audience and grovelled in a corner. It was to shock, of course, but … *and there's more*, as they say on the infomercials.

Anthony spent the weekend making hummus (good, though the chickpeas could have been cooked longer) and eating watermelon. Anthony found our veganism bemusing, but went vegan for the weekend. I respect him for that. We played cricket along the side of the house. Anthony bragged (drinking) that he'd almost played for New South Wales. Cricket is in his poems. He said that was his only thing in common with the poet Jamie Grant, a figure he loved to hate; he relished the vitriol of the arch-conservative's reviews. A case of Schadenfreude. Anthony enjoyed a nasty review, as long he wasn't on the receiving end. He was a good cricketer; he bowled a good fast ball and could even move a tennis ball off the lawn/pitch. He could belt a ball too—it was chaotic but enjoyable. You have to picture this whole process going on while he's quoting poetry (his own, others') and eyeing off your partner. He tried to bodyline me—always the sublimated aggression. You've also got to picture Anthony alone—then on the phone reading you poems a mile long, reading and reading, making you think you are the only critic, his foil, his conduit to enlightenment. Then you hear of his 'doing' the same thing with a bunch of others on the same day. Bit like changing dedications on poems to suit the girl you want to impress at the time.

That visit was the first time I'd been back in my earlier home-town Geraldton in some years and, strangely, it was as if the town wasn't there. I was upset to see that our former house—the old town hospital opposite the prison, a heritage mansion, had been bulldozed (a middle-of-the-night job) and a car park and shopping centre put in its place. We went shopping at the Coles that now stood there. I swam at St George's where I'd spent many nights camping out and trying to line up sex as a teenager, drinking under-age. But otherwise, it was just a warmish place where I went back into the pit with Anthony.

I am pretty sure it came after that visit—though it might have been done while he was still in Carnarvon—but around that time I published a chapbook of poems by Anthony and myself under my Folio (Salt) imprint. That was 1991. The first in the series was one I'd collaborated on with Philip Salom (the Western Australian poet I most respected), and this chapbook was the second. With this second one, a major contention was that I accidentally cut off the last section of one of Anthony's poems. He wasn't happy; I thought, as it turned out, that it improved the poem—but I would, wouldn't I! Fishing and blood and Hugo with a touch of Wallace Stevens (the declarative bits of) and a lot of Robert Adamson, whom we both had difficulty shaking or wiping out, anxieties of influence.

My second visit to Anthony, as I said, was somewhat more extreme. I had got into some extreme trouble in Perth with drug dealers and wanted out for a while. I'd gone cold on Anthony, in more ways than one, because he had published a poem about me using heroin. He had rung one day just after I'd scored and I kept nodding off on the phone. I sensed through the murk that he seemed both fascinated and excited by the situation. I told him to tell no one. A few weeks later a friend rang to ask if I'd read the poem in *The West Australian* newspaper by Anthony, dedicated to me. The poem's image of the floundering dugong in its narcotic swirl sent me into a rage—at being outed and at being patronised. Anthony and I didn't talk for some time. But then I wanted an escape, and Anthony was there. I'd fly to Geraldton and he'd meet me in his Toyota four-wheel drive (fishing-mobile) at the airport. I got to the Perth airport raging drunk and on amphetamines. I carried a couple of shopping bags full of sherry bottles and began arguing with a bikie in the front bar (my chosen method of suicide!). The police were called, and eventually my publisher, Ray Coffey, kindly came to collect me from the airport. The next morning I tried to fly again, in a similar condition, but sans bottles. On the plane going up, a detective was talking to another passenger about his work. I could barely resist the temptation to throw a drama for his benefit—a death wish? By the time I disembarked I was extremely agitated. Anthony met me with a bottle. I sculled whatever it was, and as we were driving past Utakarra, I threatened to climb out of the window and onto the bonnet. Anthony condemned and encouraged all at once. His gingery blond hair actually wavered, and his whiskers (never shaved properly) spiked. His shirt open, legs apart in shorts, he squeezed toes in sandals laughing sarcastically, though familiarly. He was a paradox. Seriously. He seemed in a pretty bad way himself—on anti-depressants and drinking heavily. I took my clothes off, which made him hoot, and climbed out through the car window onto the bonnet, where I perched on the roo bar 'like a gargoyle', as he said. I was painfully thin at the time, and since I'm very tall, it would have been an horrific sight. Anthony didn't slow the car down. I threw the bottle I was holding (believe it or not) back at the window, or maybe I struck the window when I crawled back in—either way, I smashed the windscreen, or cracked it. He wasn't happy about that. I was a difficult prick.

His wife was away. Things were rocky for Anthony. We weren't there for long when a girl arrived with drugs. On the television there was a porn video bought from sailors off the ships. I had a bed made up on the lounge-room floor again. I took some of Anthony's tricyclics, smoked some dope, drank. Anthony wasn't really a dope smoker—he had attracted it for me. Made him paranoid more than calm, I think. Smoked tobacco, like myself, heavily. Anthony read some of his new poems, and I quoted some of mine. We talked about American poets. He'd been corresponding with the big-reputation American poets Richard Hugo and Philip Levine and even Dickey, and was excited that they'd replied. Anthony made contact with poets via his usual technique— drinking a lot, then ringing numbers he'd tracked down and telling the poets that he was their greatest Australian fan. He did this because he was obsessive about their work—especially Hugo, who screams through his poetry of that time— but also to be part of something. Both of us knew a lot about isolation, and our compulsive behaviours were a resistance to that. We were our own worst enemies.

That stay with Anthony was more degenerate than the previous with regard to my view of my old town. I saw only bottle shops and a video store. I didn't play cricket. We argued and planned a tour away from Western Australia. We talked about wife swapping. We talked about the racism of Geraldton. Anthony is not an intellectual—in fact, he distrusts academia and theory—but he is not stupid. In many ways he is extremely bright, and he's certainly cunning.

As a writer, Anthony, it seems to me, like many of us, has always benefited from being away from larger poetry 'scenes'. A kingpin in Geraldton, he thrived on that mixture of privacy with just enough public to keep the poet ego satisfied (with excursions, phone calls, and mailing elsewhere). He loved and hated the backstabbing of the poetry world (wherever), though he provided it with plenty of fuel, and could backstab with the best of them, especially when drunk. Relatively alone, though, and with enough sex to keep him from crashing into depression (and also causing him to crash into depression), he would work with concentrated effort. Anthony loves the sound of words and is really a shamanic bard. In his work, Dylan Thomas, Gerard Manley Hopkins and other musical poets, blur with contemporary songsters like Leonard Cohen (a romantic seduction device), Billy Bragg (an absorbable social commentary), and Van Morrison … There's an obviousness, a romanticism, in all this, but the 'warp' in Anthony makes him unique and possibly a great poet. My problem with his work, and his attitude to what's possible for poetry, is that he seems to think all those deploying theory in their work are kind of taking a punt. He is suspicious, I think, of the motives of the Language poets, but still (if mockingly) tries to imitate them: what comes out looks like surrealist verse (maybe he thinks it's the same thing). I believe all poetry is political, but maybe Anthony's poetry is a case where the word itself is depoliticised. Even when he 'says' something political, the language seems separated off from a consciousness of its potential cause and effect.

On the surface, he is entirely composed of stock epithets (like, 'at the height of his powers'), but underneath he is full of fear and predation—the combination drives a socio-pathology in his poetry that makes it get under the skin.

It started on the plane heading east. Everything started. Drinking. Rivalry. Indulgence. Reading poems. I was in another Empson phase, Anthony obsessed with Dickey. Anthony thought Empson a bit of a giggle. He liked the blood in Dickey. My reply: 'Slowly the poison the whole blood stream fills. / The waste remains, the waste remains and kills.' It was 1992, early February—not long after my birthday. Playing the same old tune. Single track. Mine punk, Anthony's Leonard Cohen. We sat up the back of the plane, like the school bus. We were going across to show them. We'd see Bob Adamson, together. We agreed that if one of us ever needed the other, he'd come from no matter where. Anthony would put that to the test long after we'd gone our separate ways. I didn't go when called. I should have.

It started with chatting up the hostesses. Anthony swapped numbers and hotel contacts with them. They agreed to see us that night after the flight, but we got side-tracked. I think that night we visited a poet friend of Anthony's, and she drove us out to Anthony's father's. We behaved poorly.

The two nights we were at Anthony's dad's place were anchored by the 1992 Albertville, Canada, Winter Olympics—the last to be held in the same year as the

Summer Olympics. I loved the disparity between the cold and our heat. I realise that though I despise the Olympics they fasten my memories. 1984—Los Angeles. What happened in 1984?

1984: 7th January – 3rd March

Looking after Wheatlands. My uncle and auntie are in Europe. I was strung out late in 1983, and needed to spend time on the farm. I want to leave Australia and my uncle offers to pay me well for the work. I will fly to Paris when they return. Wheatlands farm is part of who I am. My cousins are part of who I am. They are spread around the southwest now. I feed the sheep by cradling sacks of grain on my lap and driving the motorbike slowly through the paddocks, a golden trail being latched onto behind me. A contour bank is forgotten and I lose it momentarily, pulling it back just in time. I check the water troughs, including at Hathaways a few kilometres up the track—virgin bush there. I pump water from the house dam and from the dam down near the salt for the house garden. I ride out at night in the ute and spotlight tawny frogmouths. Not to hurt them, just to watch them. I regret that kind of thing when I become vegan, as I regret shooting the ram hit by the ute on Mackie Road, its neck broken, its eyes open and still, and its faint breathing at sundown. I check gates and ride around the main block—about 9 or

10 k's, I guess. Salmon gums gleam on the edge of the salt, spreading water down through the low ground, feeding the inception of creeks. I feed the chickens and the top pigs, and reticulate a paddock of avocados—an experiment in the region. The chickens kick up a fuss at night and I take the rifle out—it's before I've made my life-oath against weapons of any kind—and, the torch held up, a fox leaps from the top of the coop ... and runs right through me. I don't pursue it. I drink beer and eat watermelon and C. visits me. We watch cricket—the reception is sketchy and the television runs off a booster, 32 volts from the generator out in the pumping shed. We drop acid and the stars implode. I hear the animals loudly and don't want to eat them. Alone again, a strange peace envelops me. I ride the motorbike naked and Terry drives up and doesn't bat an eyelid (cousin by marriage who likes poetry, what do you expect?). 'Going to be hot today ... all okay? You managing?' No worries. 'Saw you wandering out on the salt last week ... came to see if you needed a hand. Nothing much down there. Just salt. And it gets bloody hot—like mirrors. Like an oven.' I like its heat. It has its own quietness.

Late March – May

Europe. Arrive Paris. Head to Denmark. See fire-eaters and am reminded of Lasseter's Reef. Meet

M. of the young socialist league and follow him to
Helsinki. Train from Copenhagen to Paris. The
former lover of the Russian-born structural linguist
Roman Jakobson (1896–1982) is beautiful at eighty.
We drink beer and I sleep in her lap. She reads my
small book of poems—*The Frozen Sea*. She says: 'Yes,
it's from a line of Kafka's …' I love her. Easter in
Notre Dame. To Germany, Switzerland, Italy. The air
force general's son is still with me—he told me in
Munich it would be an initiation. I laughed to myself
and the landlady kicked up a stink. Lost him in
Venice. Brindisi and drunk. Waiting. More cops.
Greece. Girl my own age not wanting to be left late at
night in Athens. I walk away and find one of my
homes. Later, the Lion's Gate, bums on seats and
whether women attended the nearby theatre.
Probably not, and it bothered me. Samos. Pythagoras.
Turkey. Epidaurus. Selcuck. Istanbul and the black
market. A getaway. Greece. Arrested at Patris, suspected of couriering drugs from Turkey. I'd made a
rapid escape from Istanbul after being accused of ille-
gally changing Greek drachma into Turkish lira …
after dragging me out of a crowd and driving me to
the interrogation rooms with the muzzles of sub-
machine guns, they told me it was because of the
recent Turkish stamp in my passport (gained on entry
into Turkey). Full body search. Eventually, London.
The Thames. A river connecting to the rivers I've
known always. Paris. Perth, Australia.

June–October

C.'s place in South Perth. Stoned. Drunk. Underground nightclub. Mixing the slow and the quick. C. reading and re-reading Machiavelli's *The Prince*. Hitching to Port Hedland. Meeting the 'crew'—C.'s Main Roads workmates from his time up there. I think we dropped in to see my father in Carnarvon while hitching back. Before this, I was last in the red iron-ore dust town of Port Hedland with my dad. As a teenager. They'd found a body a few days before we arrived—out the back of the pub where dad took us so he could drink. The carriers lined up off the coast. A strike. There were constant dramas. The house got trashed to the Sex Pistols. It was a polite neighbourhood. C.'s pet cat was named Misha, after the mascot of the 1980 Soviet (Moscow) Olympics—the one the Americans (and others) didn't go to because of the Soviet invasion of Afghanistan … The cat didn't watch the Los Angeles Olympics: July 28th through August 12th. The winter in the southern hemisphere—in Perth at least—was not harsh. The cat was gentle and soothing to have around. The Americans seemed hypocrites, their idea of freedom as retarded as the Soviets'. Capitalism dressed up as liberty is capitalism by any other name. Time has proved this angry summation. All nation states are wrong. Centralised government is wrong. Free enterprise, through corporations, becomes just a different form of centralisation. Steps towards forms of resistance. A march on the Western

Australian Parliament in support of indigenous land rights. A protest in the swampland behind Murdoch University against land development. Things get heavy there—clearers have a go at protesters, as do cops. Overnight, somebody sugars the tanks of bull-dozers. Direct action becomes an obsession. Within a year, committed activism against racist nationalists (removal of their racist propaganda), speaking against their activities, will segue into anti-imperialist activities. Writing letters of protest for Jim, militant metal workers' unionist. Against the US funding of the Contras, against the activities of the Seventh Fleet, the existence of nuclear weapons and nuclear power, against apartheid. C. is committed ideologi-cally but doesn't want trouble. Wants to avoid being arrested. He will be elsewhere when it reaches that point. We both decide we have to get out. Overland to Europe. Indonesia, Malaysia, Thailand, Burma. Bangladesh, India, Nepal ... all the way, we plan. For as long as it takes. Apply for the 'wheat bins' through CBH (Co-operative Bulk Handling)—do the courses. Take the tests. Come November I am a pro-tein sampler at Mingenew a few hundred k's away. C. at a bin about sixty k's inland from there.

November – late December

Persecution in the living quarters at the wheat bins is extreme. 'Pom' especially cops it—a half-alive snake in his bed. My genitals crunched in the shower. Beer. Whiskey. Acid dropped on the tower. The extreme heat goading them on. Afrikaner truck-driver bragging of using an AK-47 to shoot 'Kaffirs' collecting water; he praises apartheid and finds plenty of support among farmers, drivers, bin workers. It burns deep and you will later be among those who flash mirrors to stop cricketers playing who have supported the regime. It's a violence you can't defend now, but the passion behind the protest is the same. Header hitting stone, sparking, and sending a few thousand acres up in smoke. Fire ban. No smoking near the grid—ever! Reading Conrad—the sea of wheat. Rosie and her girlfriend fucking everybody in the hut—some are 'mercy fucks'. Hauled over the pool table, naked. Guy with daughters by his daughters by his daughters. High-powered guns. They did kittens. Cats. All non-human life. Human life disposed of at the bar. 'Black fellas" tin huts shot up after the Friday booze-up. You scream in protest and are beaten within an inch of your life. Escape and hide in the scrub. Hitch back to Perth and write for your last cheque. And these are the facts.

What was Anthony doing in 1984? Six years older than me—possibly doing his studies. No doubt singing songs. Maybe finding Robert Adamson. Yes, hanging around the Poetry Society. Conjecture.

The Winter Olympics amused us because of the curling. Anthony's fascination with this surreal activity began then because it was an exhibition sport for that year—two Olympics later it became an official Olympic sport. He'd say (and it turned up in a poem later) 'the ancient art of curling'—and crack up. It had an element of Monty Python for him.

Anthony's father, when we went to see him, was an enigma to me and, I, I think, to him. I liked him, though thought he was a pretty tough bloke. I'd never really heard Anthony talk about him, but I got a sense of him through Anthony's first book of poems, *Dreaming in Stone*. (For example: 'My father could whistle up a fox / with the bent lid of a jam tin.'—'Whistling Fox'). Anthony had mainly mentioned his mother. And was there a stepfather? Who was it that had to deal with the police when Anthony as a youth managed to burn a building down? He had a few scrapes over the years.

I remember Anthony stayed in the Beaufort Hotel backpackers', one night when he couldn't go home, for some reason. There were also plenty of nights when I didn't go home. Mixing memories. I do know, as an aside, that at the Beaufort early opener where I often drank, I was playing pool with a guy who started telling me he'd murdered someone that night at the Chelsea Tavern in Nedlands. That it was more like manslaughter, but the cops would find him soon and lock him up. His girlfriend sat at the table drinking something like tequila sunrises. I drank straight tequila and gave him a copy of one of my books of poetry, which, like Anthony, I would carry around in my bag. We'd carry around copies of our latest books no matter how far gone we were—as affirmation, proof of an existence outside addiction (for me, at least), to give away, to have someone read us, to read ourselves and feel bad about what we should have done, to resent and reject publication, then hunger for it all over again.

Anthony's father seemed the rural connection in Anthony's poetry—maybe he was a stock salesman or livestock realtor or auctioneer. Maybe how Anthony found himself working in the country, thinking up horrors like the poem 'Cro-kill'. His father drove a big car and dressed the country man in the city fashion I am familiar with. Sydney or the bush. He'd recently remarried, if I recall, though his wife was only there in a gentle, shadowy way. I remember him advising us on how to be good young men. On how we'd lost the plot with the poetry vocation bit. He spoke to me on the side about his worries regarding Anthony's choices in life. And our drinking. He dropped us at the airport when we flew to Wagga Wagga. Or he dropped us somewhere away from his place. I remember the back of the car.

We attended the NSW Writers' Centre Festival, where Anthony told me that a prescription-drugged magazine editor, who seemed to stare at me whenever we met and to get too close for my liking, had asked him why I always put my hands in my lap when I sat, or held my books in front of my crotch. Insecurity? Self-consciousness? Both, I imagine, he replied, or something to that effect. He enjoyed it. She continued to stare at me.

Anthony disappeared with women on a few occasions. The women always looked dishevelled when they returned slightly later, or ahead of him. People remarked on it. We did our readings in the formulaic way that'd get us through—we knew our programme and our sideshow, and we stuck to it. We fed off each other, reinforced each other. We were a team. The jealousies were on hold, or deployed elsewhere, deflected. What was said behind the scenes, I don't know. I think Anthony saw himself as assisting in my poetic coming out. I certainly didn't see it that way. This was his home turf and he knew everyone. I received lots of advice on how not to try too hard to get ahead. Don't be demonstrative, don't publish too much, pull your head in. The event annoyed me—the little rituals of behaviour so as not to offend egos when the whole event was about ego, and about clapping and laughing at comrades' and supporters' jokes and speaking snidely about those who were of no use, or had got out of line: repulsive. One great thing was hearing an eminent Korean poet read. Nothing for him to gain, nothing for him to prove; though I don't doubt the pattern of such events brings the same gamesmanship in South Korea.

Anthony and I flew to Wagga Wagga. I would fly out on my own a couple of days later and head straight back to my then partner. We settled into our hotel, then spent a few hours downstairs playing the pokies, to which Anthony introduced me in the New South Wales sense of things. I'd played them before, elsewhere in the world, but generally avoided gambling—one of my few resistances. Not long before, I had blown most of the family's money by placing a large bet on a roulette wheel during my only-ever visit to the Burswood Casino. On that occasion I'd been thrown out of Connections nightclub in Perth, been sexually assaulted across the bonnet of one taxi and escaped in another whose driver, on our arrival at the casino (I'd asked to go 'anywhere'), offered me the lift free if I gave him a head job. When I refused, he followed me into the casino and hung around. Three in the morning. So, I bet thousands on thirteen. It came up three times in a row. I—we—were rich. I lost the lot on the fourth spin. Having no money, I snagged a phone call to a drug dealer who came and picked me up and supplied a few grams of hash on credit (I was always good for it, whatever the trauma caused in obtaining it) and drove me home to Westfield up near Armadale, in the far outer suburbs. He showed me his new pistol, loose in his glove-box, with a box of spare ammunition.

But back to Wagga Wagga: the pokies got me going and I lost a fair bit of loose change. We went out and ate falafel rolls—Anthony knew the town. I could get vegan food there. Once again, he was good that way. We sat by the river talking over the reading that night, and relationships he'd had with people in the town, including an actress there. We sat looking into the river and both felt shithouse—severe hangovers. I am not sure if it was the following day, but we also did a radio interview with the ABC. It would be interesting to hear that tape—playing the out-of-town authorities come to illuminate the locals. The reading was bad—I know, because I was sick with drink. I wanted back to the hotel. Somehow I'd got hold of a bunch of Serepax or

Valium—maybe from Bob Adamson in Sydney—and ate the lot. Was it eight or thirty-eight? It finished me off, and Anthony apparently had to ring the hospital. I remember saying to him, when we'd been discussing getting some prostitutes to the room, that we could just do it for free ourselves—then passing out. I have vague recollections—probably more detail than he'd like to think.

The prostitutes must have come between the pub and the pills. Anthony was with 'his' in the bed next to me, while I fumbled and talked and tried to stop hallucinating. The woman I was with was interesting, so in that clichéd way—and not for the first time—I asked her to go outside with me and talk. And we did. About Aboriginality and Wagga. About racism and prostitution. 'In the end, mate, they just want to stick it into anyone. Bastards.' As was I. I told her how I'd once gone out with a 'working girl'—briefly. It hadn't worked out. She left me because I was too out of control; she was perfectly in control. Anthony didn't believe it but I know I didn't have sex with the prostitute in Wagga, though I did pay well. There, the disclaimer. Anthony must have talked about this incident, as complaints (unfounded) were made to the Australia Council about us misspending our grant money. One poet in particular, declaring his hatred of the Australia Council, professed to hate our debauchery even more and 'told' on us. Back seat of the bus. Boys' Own Annual. School. I was an immaculate student at school. The next morning I was out of there and heading back home.

I saw Anthony once more when I was with my then partner—at a Christmas party at his wife's parents' place over near one of the northern beaches. I listened to New Order's *Blue Monday,* which I'd brought on tape, over and over, stoned. I was always stoned and drunk. We played cricket—Anthony and I—briefly in the dark, down the side of the house. New Order, Joy Division—fascists to me then, as now. It was a perverse thing to do.

I remember Anthony saying to me of the poet Tracy Ryan that he thought her incredibly beautiful. I didn't know he'd been involved with her for some time, and that pretty well sums up the nature of our friendship, and maybe all friendships with Anthony. Things are separated, compartmentalised. It feels as if you are only a friend so far, as a specific entertainment. Fair-weather. I replied, regarding Tracy Ryan whom I barely knew, that I didn't think so particularly. I remember I did think so particularly, but didn't want to go there—I was already having enough trouble preserving my decaying relationship with my then partner …

It actually wasn't that long after that discussion that Tracy crossed my path again at a reading, and then I rang her a couple of times (out of it), and then gradually convinced her to come and see me in my South Perth flat, where I was living apart from my partner. This was a bad-flat scenario. I wrote my thirtieth birthday poem then, and that pretty well sums it up.

It was more than twelve months, and after my relation-ship of the time fell apart, before Tracy and I connected again and began a life (of sorts) together. I was battling severe heroin addiction by that stage; half of our first year together was spent with me scoring, and the other half with me on prescribed Doloxene, and even stronger drugs, trying to straighten out. I was worse on those drugs than on smack, though it was easier to get them. I won't dredge through the shit and horrors and ODs of that year, but where the story really goes awry is when Tracy and I go to do a residency in the Blue Mountains early in 1996 and cross Anthony's path as a couple. That's when the sparks flew and things got serious. It was the end of any vestigial friendship we had left.

There's one postscript before larger postscripts to this story. A localised postscript. We attended a quiz night— I hate them. Anthony was on the neighbouring table with some of his friends. The competition between the tables was palpable, though none professed to care. It was an unpleasant evening. Anthony got drunk; we remained sober. And so we parted. I have not seen him since, and nei-ther has Tracy. In our next life, the incarnation of 'hawk wind'—or, as I called him affectionately, 'ant'—was on the e-mail, until that too went silent, was sucked into the black hole of nothingness. Becalmed in fair weather.

Anthony is now considered to be a major poet in Australia, not only via accusations of the dreaded self-promotional skills which are pointed his way as much as mine, but because other poets read him.

I have a lasting picture of Anthony in my head: dark sunnies (wrap-around), deploying the low rumbling voice of persuasion, then switching to another listening and saying he can't stand 'the jealous carping of the poetry world', and then laughing about someone needing to put on their 'flak jacket' because of a bad review. Watching Anthony at readings, I always felt he feared what he couldn't understand sensually. He needed to feel it to like it. And sometimes his feelings were dulled by depression, substances, and creative gaps … then he wandered, a troubadour back on the road, looking for a home base and imaginary security to store his poems.

He writes of death with intensity, if without delicacy; he pries where he shouldn't, and he can seem tasteless and disrespectful; but when he says 'it's all for the poetry', we can—partly—believe him.

5

Helsinki

M. IS TELLING ME that Brecht wrote at this table at Helsinki railway station, back in 1940, during his long exile from Nazi Germany. He also stayed on a country estate while in Finland, but I'd like to think he did some of his work on the play *Mr Puntila and his Man Mutti* at this table. When I was there in 1984, I wrote a poem about it but I can't find the draft I did at that time.

How did I get there? It's something of a haze, but I first met M. on a train from Hamburg to Copenhagen. He sat down next to me, leant back and watched me reading. You like poetry? he asked. I am a poet, I replied, not quite confident in this claim, though not knowing what else I could say, or what else I might be. Do you write political poetry? he asked. I am an anarchist, I replied, so I guess everything I write is political. He asked to see some of my poems and I showed him a copy of *The Frozen Sea*, which he read slowly, deliberately. I got stuck on one line in my book and looked at him over the top of the page: fair, clipped hair, round glasses like Lenin's (my first thought), dressed as a 'worker'. I have just been at the Hamburg Socialist Youth Group camp, he said, handing me back my small book of poems. I am a Trotskyite, he continued. I laughed. What's the problem? You look like a blond Lenin. He laughed. Your poems aren't political, he said. Not like Brecht, anyway. You should come to Helsinki and see where Brecht wrote before he went to Russia. Before he went to America. In America they grilled him for being a communist. And so the conversation went, all the way to Copenhagen, where we agreed to meet up again in Stockholm the next day. I wandered around Copenhagen and watched child fire-eaters and in my head wrote the first lines of my Lasseter poems, which would later appear in my book *Night Parrots*:

A troupe of fire-eaters
stumbled on Lasseter's Reef

For seven days and nights
they entertained

throwing vast jets of flame
out over desert ...

The linking of northern cold, snow, and desolation of whiteness with the 'full emptiness' of Australian desert began early in my writing. I met M. in Stockholm the next day and he crashed out on the floor of my hotel, the Anno Domini, both of us drunk, the window open in freezing weather. Or was it someone else I met that I crashed out with?

M. continued on to Helsinki by train, while I caught the ferry through the Baltic: the islands in the morning light, heavy as dreadnoughts, have stayed with me. The islands were surrounded by small and large craft, including old sailing boats of superb craftsmanship, golden in a black dawn. I tried to write what I saw, the sky fused to the islands fused to the water … I was reminded of lines from the Finnish epic poem *The Kalevala*:

> The old Väinämöinen said:
> 'As I was carving a boat
> was working on a new craft
>   I needed three words
>   to round off the stern
>   and to raise the prow;
> when I could get them nowhere
> not find them on lands, in skies
> I must come to Tuonela
>   go to Death's abodes
>   where I'd get those words
>   learn those mysteries.'[6]

Bound down with duty-free shopping, tired locals and tourists pumped the slot machines on the upper deck of the towering ocean-going ferry, their all night marathon binge

6 *Keith Bosley (trans)*, The Kalevala, *Oxford World Classics, 1989, p. 196.*

glass-windowing the Baltic half-light, their partners crashed out in the cheapest aeroplane-style seats at the bow-end of the deck.

M. was there to meet me. We stored my bag at the station, then went to Brecht's café to get a hot drink, wandered around the city examining the block architecture, 'cold and pitiless and governmental' by M.'s own definition, then made our way to his place on the outskirts of Helsinki. Finland wasn't as well off in the early 1980s as it would later become, and the effects of the Cold War were stronger there than most places. However, M.'s house was luxurious.

Finland had fought the Russians during the Second World War (the Winter War and Continuation War) and, regardless of Brecht and others fleeing there from the Nazis, was associated with the Axis powers. Finland had feigned neutrality but co-operated with the Germans. It saw this as a necessity for survival—caught between two large military powers—to play the power and appeasement game. Its wars with the Soviet Union were in many ways independent of the larger power plays going on at the time. During the Cold War, there was the desire to tread between conflicting forces—a policy of 'neutrality' to preserve Finnish democracy expressed itself through non-alignment. But geography placed Finland at an important crossover point for agents and clandestine dialogues. The perception of a liminal zone (commentators discuss the difference between buffer state and 'grey zone') was commonplace. All this is, unfortunately, relevant to this diversion …

M.'s father—his mother was not in the picture—was away for work. He was a businessman. M.'s brother, when we arrived, was sitting in the living area listening to Jimi Hendrix. I had bought a bottle of duty-free Johnny Walker Red Label on the ferry and we all started drinking. M. wanted to get naked in the sauna, to introduce me to the Finnish custom of the hot and cold: emerging from the steam to chill down rapidly in the snow. I crashed out drunk in the sauna, fully clothed.

In the evening we went into the city to drink at an underground students' club. Very drunk, I stood on a table and yelled poetry. M. told me I could have any girl there I wanted. Why? I asked. Because I am the May King here, and they will believe me when I say you're a special kind of guy. I felt nervous and hid this behind even more exuberant and extreme behaviour. Sculling competitions, recitations, nihilist bravado. I will take you to a German play being performed in Finnish, which I will translate for you into English as chance permits, M. said. We went to *Brecht on Brecht* performed by an experimental student theatre group. I learnt more about theatre from not speaking the language than I would have if I'd understood everything. Brecht was Brecht, regardless. Like when I first read *Baal* on the farm, two years before. Baal was out there, shooting up forty-four gallon drums and foxes, and making disturbed poetry of it. A romantic implosion. Then back to the student bar for last drinks. Pick a woman, said M., insistent. I felt ridiculous. You can't pick someone like that, I said. It's kind of sick. We do that here, he said, as if it were a cultural necessity (it's not), and I'd be betraying Finnish custom if I didn't! I tarried. M 'picked' for me. You are going home with O. The story of O.?, I thought. And so I did ...

O. is as tall as I am—and I am around six–three—with aggressive hair and a bomber jacket. She is about twenty-five, I am twenty. She talks incessantly about Jimi Hendrix. What is it with Helsinki and Hendrix? She says she likes the Communist Party and fucking, in that order. She has fucked rock musicians and playwrights, but no poets yet. She feels it a duty to broaden her literary horizons. She herself doesn't write, but considers herself a 'critic'. I am too pissed to care what her mark for me might be. We bus right out into the suburbs. I have been wound through the labyrinth. Her place is in an apartment block—just a couple of rooms. A mattress on the floor, spirits bottles, ashtrays, guitar, picture of Hendrix like the one I had on the back of my door when I first came down from the country to go to university ...

We prop ourselves against the wall, on the bed, and drink and smoke. She offers some opium—I have not had it before, and think it's really weird to be having it in Helsinki. She prepares a pipe and heats the opium with a flame so the smoke wreathes out and is sucked back. It's a slow, nauseous stone. We start to undress and the door opens and a white Finnish Hendrix look-a-like, right down to skin-tight purple pants, big belt and neck chains, appears. He starts to undress and climb onto the mattress. I am not as broadminded as I will later become, and drag myself to my feet. Hey man, I'm not into that ... They laugh. You've drunk our booze and smoked our drugs, and now you want to bale out. You're no fucking poet, adds O. I stumble towards the door and out into the night. At first, I think it's about eleven at night, but it is more likely two or three in the morning. I am freezing, though strangely warm inside. I wander in a cushioned daze.

A car pulls over. Two guys—'straights' (they look like civil servants)—are in the front. The passenger leans back and opens the back door and motions for me to get in. I have no idea why I do but I do. Warmth? They start to drive and say nothing. And they drive and drive and drive. We seem to be doing the rounds of the suburbs. It feels like hours pass. I try to speak with them, but they don't reply. I have my Swiss Army knife, bought recently near St Stephen's in Vienna, in my pocket. I am clutching it. One of them says in English, Give me your passport. I do. He keeps it. Where have you been? To a party. Where? I don't (honestly) know. Why? I was invited. They drive until daybreak. I am dozing on the back seat, then jerking awake with fear. They are talking to me about politics. They ask if I have been to the Soviet Union. Strangely, I was talking with M. earlier about doing a run with him to Leningrad; but I say nothing. They ask if I am 'sympathetic' to Communism. I say I am. We have reached the station. I have told them my bag is stored there. I have no idea why I am telling total strangers anything, but I feel compelled. They escort me out of the car to the locker, which they open with the key I provide, hand me my bag, and say, leave Finland on the next ferry. I ask if I can make a phone call. Yes. I call M., who takes a long time to answer the phone. The weirdoes are watching me, just out of earshot. I tell M. what's happened and he says, Shit, man, you've got to leave—don't tell them anything about me. I will meet you, though, by the ferry.

I am walked to the port, where I am given back my passport, and await the opening of the ticket office—I have a Eurail pass, so it's just a matter of registering. Seemingly satisfied, my new friends leave. I don't know if they are watching. I stay seated. M. finds me a couple of hours later. He slides next to me and hugs me. You have been picked up by the special police, he says. The secret police. You must leave. I am totally confused. Within minutes M. is gone and I am left with only his name and phone number in a diary I kept in my pocket and didn't show the strangers. His name I will give to my eldest son as a middle name. I will speak once more with M., years later, when another friend gets jealous after hearing the story and rings that number to check the veracity of my story. I have never been back to the Grey Zone.

6

He always called me 'Johnno' or 'Jack'

JOHN FORBES had a way of resting an elbow on any available surface and holding his drink high in the other hand. If you stayed with him, he was different in the morning—hair tousled, and still in his black t-shirt. In a lethargic and semi-sarcastic way he'd light his Camel, brew strong coffee, shake his head and look for a newspaper. I've written a few pieces over the years about my tensions with John—how I felt he said one thing to me and the opposite to the next person who crossed his path. The level of hurt was a measure of my affection and respect for him.

John always inexplicably thought his steel-rimmed square glasses cooler than mine, which were 'nod-off glasses': large lenses, thick frame, secured by a cord. Like me, John cleaned his smeary lenses on his black t-shirt. Most often, in my experience, he wore black jeans. His hair was usually short, which helped with bike-riding—passion and necessity: he didn't drive. Having been brought up in the tropics—his father an air force meteorologist (meteorology subtexts his poems, like the metaphysicals' spheres)—John preferred the heat, even the humidity, to the cold. He was a solid man who liked to think he looked after himself, which he generally didn't. He would mention the names of past girlfriends, artist friends, fellow poets, regularly. He saw himself as part of a community, or communities, divided primarily between Sydney, his home of choice, and Melbourne, his home of circumstance (which was also partially a home of choice). He liked pubs and conversation. He smoked his filterless Camels to the very end. He tilted back his head, dragging smoke, and laughed a laugh that ran into a hacking cough. His eyes were piercing and sarcastic. He pretty well retained his dark hair colour. His body didn't work as well as he wanted.

John satirised Australia but was incredibly nationalistic, even to the point of militaristic patriotism. Though he dissected nationalism, he was so clearly *of* it. He was a rebelliously 'proud Australian', who would mock the official language of nation. For him, true nation evolved out of the ratbaggery, out of the larrikin, out of the 'digger' resistance to authority. He saw himself as a rebel who'd been tamed a little (though he would always like to point out that such and such a line would preserve his 'street cred'. One has to remember that, with John Forbes, irony can rarely be separated from sincerity, and vice versa).

John believed in a kind of class 'labourism' and a revenge against the wealthy and successful; that the Australian nation he worshipped was built out of the have-nots, that the principles of the fair go and mateship were honourable. One could point to numerous examples of his mocking such beliefs; yet if we look closer, we see that he mocks false and duplicitous applications, he mocks insincerity and the abuse of myth—but not the myths themselves. He saw himself as an honest witness to what it was (and was not) to be Australian, and in many ways it's why he stayed an Australian poet, despite the Americanisms (New York School, cut and dried) in his writing. He took the loose affiliation of Harvard poets and friends: Ashbery, Koch, Schuyler and O'Hara; took them into Sydney and later Melbourne, and reinvented them with the day-to-day trappings of televisual Australia.

I find it difficult, if not impossible, to write about John Forbes with any clarity or distance. He would ironise my sincerity, should I display it, yet be disappointed if it wasn't there. He could convince you that his damnations never included you, but you knew you were in there too. The writing style should be sharp and witty, and praise should be moderate so it in fact has more impact. These contradictions fed not only our relationship but John's relationship with the world at large.

John craved recognition because poetry was what he was good at; he felt that if he didn't get praise there, he'd get it nowhere—that, in a sense, his life would be wasted. He set himself up as a mentor figure to me, and I let him.

The reasons for this were subterranean, from both points of view, but despite all that has been said since his death, we had a genuinely close and even confidential friendship. I was surprised to find that, even at the time I was most distanced from the world, when I removed myself to the Cocos Islands in 1994/95, he directed a fax and a bunch of poems (one unpublished to this day, others different versions of earlier poems) to me: 'To John Kinsella: West Island Lodge, Cocos Islands'. He probably got the address from my mother, with whom he was in regular contact. I don't know if Mum ever rang him more than once or twice, but I do know that he regularly rang her in the early hours of the morning to discuss his personal life, his assessment of my dramas and situation, poetry, and anything else that crossed his mind. He was usually under the weather.

I recall once when I was living in the apartments (as the owners preferred to call them) opposite the Perth Zoo, and in a really bad way. I'd lost my temper in traffic in what amounted to a road rage incident. I'd yelled and shrieked and stopped my car at traffic lights, berating an 'idiot' for going through a red light. My mother must have mentioned it to John because he rang me (just before the phone was cut off), telling me to cool it … to get the drinking, drugging and temper under control. But it was all of this that attracted John. His problems often seemed mild, he'd say, by comparison. Of course, they weren't.

John Forbes's visit to Perth in 1991 changed me from a fairly solitary poet who had relatively little contact with the 'literary world' to one who frequented readings and mixed with poets on more regular (if still rare at this stage) occasions. Here was a poet who was also 'out of it', even out of control at times. But it's not the self-image John had, and he felt that he could, even if ironically, be something of a role model for me. He tolerated what he saw as my overdrive and dangerous enthusiasm because my downtimes were so absolutely down. We kind of became addicted to each other. It was a fusion of near yet distant generations— he was only thirteen years older than me. As time went on and I published more, and became more 'public', John felt as if the demons of success had got me, and that, while he needed to bag me to his mates for 'ambition' and 'careerism', he felt quiet words in my ear about my behaviour would help me avoid the worst of this, the true fate of banality through professionalism. In a letter he later wrote to me in Cambridge in 1997, he said: 'There is much you need me to talk with you about but "talk" is the operative word—it canna be done via letters, faxes or even E-mails. So I am looking forward to seeing you in September ...'

John's visit to Tracy and me in Churchill College, Cambridge University, had been eagerly and apprehensively awaited. He could be pleasant and nasty in one breath. Which John would arrive, or would both? The knock at the door of our Churchill College flat was erratic. John, dressed like Johnny Cash without the hat and wearing desert boots, or the like—walked inside, tramping fenland mud over the collegiate carpet, and tin-soldiered onto the lounge. (Tracy—not house-proud—reminds me that he apologised for the mud, and did it again every time he came in: 'Oops. Sorry, Trace.') I had just bought a *Best of the Ramones* CD to celebrate his arrival, put it on, and he leapt up and started pogoing around the room. It's the thing that our then five-year-old daughter remembers most distinctly about him. He was pretty crook, coughing and gasping for air a lot. Within nine or ten months he'd be dead.

Though he was doing a residency at Loughborough further north, John spent as much time as possible in Cambridge. He wanted to belong, but his feeling that he *didn't* belong was such that he had to be there to mock it. He got off on the smart kids. He loved their naivety. He could play a poet–mentor role here. And he was, he felt, smart enough. (He was.) He was bemused how I'd gone from total drug addict out-of-control fuck-up, to entirely sober 'over-publishing' Cambridge functionary.

The funny thing about being in Cambridge was that I always felt comfortable being there—at the college and university, at least. Living in England as an Australian—or as any kind of foreigner—can be alienating, but I felt secure and cloistered in a place of learning. Once, as a teenager, I went through a period of believing I had a spiritual vocation and even discussed with the Anglican Bishop of Perth going to Cambridge to study theology! I went down a slightly different path in life … but Cambridge always seemed the place to go to get work done, which is why I went there really.

Attending a seminar I gave about pastoral poetry in Australia, he loudly said the opposite to what I said at every opportunity. He might have been right. Walking along outside the Møller Centre (where we had put him up in the college for a week—he'd written to us from Australia that he wanted to stay with us to kick his addictions before going up to start his residency in Loughborough, and the Centre seemed a good, safe place for this), he told me that if he wanted to, he could destroy me, take everything I have, reduce me to non-poet. I told him he couldn't. Not now, maybe, he said, but I *could have*. The struggle was on. It has always amazed me about myself that, though I had little to do with the 'boys' at school, and in fact was routinely beaten up by them and accused of non-male-type behaviour, and though I politically loathed it, I also played the game in my own way. Be against competitiveness and you become competitive anyway. And that's the relationship I ended up having with Anthony Lawrence, and why it had to stop. It's why my relationship with John, as the mentoring decayed, became so difficult.

There were two incidents I've discussed elsewhere that stick in my mind from John's regular visits to Cambridge. He developed a friendship with an Anglican minister and would stay in his house on the outskirts of Cambridge. He would then go to student parties or meet with us, or others. One was the night he got into a fight at a disco in Loughborough—I won't go into it again—and the other was about his frustration over one of the Cambridge PhD students he sort of found attractive. She became a useful foil in our battle: he'd quote her against me. On one occasion we met in the market square early on a Saturday morning and he had a bad hangover. We sat on the edge of an ancient stone fountain and he told me of his arguments and triumphs at a party where Keston Sutherland, Andrea Brady and other young Cambridge poets had been. I could tell he was uneasy about the impression he'd made. When it got to that stage, he'd start giving me a 'lesson' on how to behave in Cambridge. I said something ironic like 'you can't be a dickhead here and get away with it' and red rag to a bull that it was: he bit. In his great late poem '3 Songs for Charles Darwin' he wrote:

> 'You know what's wrong
> with this place?'
> of Cambridge, England, John Kinsella said,
> 'you can't be a dickhead here,
> not for a moment!'
>   'Well' reply
> 6 generations plus ring-ins plus me
> 'You can always try' ...[7]

A beautiful rejoinder, an about-face that condemns and participates. Of course, John never wanted to be seen as a dickhead anywhere, but he'd kick against the pricks and prove them dickheads by his superior (Australian/colonial) intelligence and experience. It was a challenge. But he wanted their approval—it was like watching a centre/periphery implosion, a head-banging blast against the 'ancient stone'.

'Love' (rather than 'love') was always John's issue, and it was an ideal in his Catholic Madonna–whore world that

---

7 *from John Forbes,* Collected Poems: 1970–1998, *Brandl & Schlesinger, Rose Bay, NSW, n.d., pp. 251–6.*

could never be satisfied. In that way, my partner (wife), like many other unavailable women, became John's 'target' on one occasion—only one. He tried it on her because he knew she wouldn't respond … He said to her: 'I've often thought that if you weren't with the beanpole you might be with *me*.' Tracy replied: 'I love the beanpole, John.' 'Yeah,' he said, 'I know, I'm only joking … Well, I'm not *really* joking.' Tracy says she remembers this verbatim because his wit was always so sharp that it seemed as if it had to be rehearsed and yet clearly came on the spur of the moment. A bottle of whiskey down, and his brain was still in linguistic overdrive.

Going back further, John's visit to Perth in 1991 was, in my experience, primarily about scoring 'glug' (cough medicine). We'd been corresponding or speaking on the phone for about six months, if I recall. A few days before, he had arrived in Perth for a residency. I'd picked him up from his accommodation, at his request, and driven him to three different pharmacies (from Canning Highway, South Perth, to Stirling Highway, Mosman Park) so he could buy over-the-counter cough syrup (containing a mixture of codeine phosphate and ephedrine). He basically sculled the bottles. I offered him some of the 'heavier stuff' I was into, but he said that though he'd injected a few times, it wasn't his scene. 'Glug' suited him just right. The contradiction at work. Upper and downer at once. (He once wrote a great poem about 'scoring' Actifed CC in London.) He gave me a copy of his 'bicentennial book' *The Stunned Mullet* the same day: I was amazed when he said it had sold almost two thousand copies. It was a bicentennial project, he quipped ... he felt slightly guilty that it was financed by a programme feeding on the dispossession of Aboriginals, but he liked the sales. He told me he'd rarely ever met any Aboriginals. I wasn't sure what he was getting at.

John was fascinated and disturbed when I told him that a friend had taken to drinking on the balcony of a hotel in Perth, almost opposite a bookshop, because he liked to admire from a distance a young woman who worked in the store. John thought he'd try it out. I think he did. He certainly spoke with the woman on more than one occasion and was fascinated by her. 'Another one I can't have ...' was the gist of his comments. When, a year or so later, I published *Salt* magazine issues 3 and 4, they included John's poem for her. The last lines summed up his much-discussed problem of being repellent to those he desired most while also admiring the 'refusal' (I doubt he ever actually 'asked'):

Anti-Romantic[8]

You meet your daemon &
respond with contempt

for all depth & poetry
driven by love & breath

self-conscious bitterness
is best, besides lust or a

8 *ibid., p. 162.*

detached disgust—as
long as there's nothing

hysterical about it Art
& life both require this

but your attitude like
inspiration disappears,

leaves you ugly & stranded,
the moment you admire it

The pronoun cuts both ways. It was the loved and beloved, the infatuated and rejected that interested John.

In 1993, I published John Forbes's chapbook *troubador* [*sic*] with Folio. The Folio pamphlets I published between 1990 and 1995 were printed on high-quality wheat paper in limited editions of two hundred with fifty or a hundred signed and numbered by the author. Though they were designed on an Apple Mac Classic, the poems and frames for the pages were printed out on a laser printer and pasted into sheets for printing at the local Snap Printers. They lived between desktop publishing and the old way of doing things. This may account for their tactility and, I think, beauty. I was influenced by French poetry publications when designing them: just text on the cover, with a coloured frame around it. With John's chapbook, we went for a reddish frame and strong black-ink text. The benefit of these chapbooks was that they allowed poets to think of poems between books. John actually wrote a number of the poems, including the title poems and his brilliant 'Ode to Karl Marx', specifically for (or, rather, spurred on by) the prospect of the chapbook. A non-profit making project, the 'sub' nature of it in particular appealed to John:

> Old father of the horrible bride whose
> wedding cake has finally collapsed, you
>
> spoke the truth that doesn't set us free ...[9]

Making use of what I call the 'articulated line' and an enjambment that ironises the ode form, the poem in the chapbook (brightly framed on beautiful paper) ironises even its own appearance.

I always felt a Forbes book should be small, and the to-ing and fro-ing over contents and drafts for this tiny booklet bespeak a much larger creative process. I had the feeling these were given out as pieces of pain, pride, failed 'love tokens', and conversation. What is often forgotten about Forbes's poems, because of their wit and irony, their Augustan subversion of the lyric, is that they were most often odes and songs. The most ironic of his odes is also a celebration of the art. And Forbes thought of himself as a singer: as a troubadour. He wrote razzos to his own tales of chivalry and paradox, undercutting himself but still engaging with a contradictory set of emotions. How to be a barfly and a singer of poised lines. The booklet ends with 'song' from his poem 'Sydney':

9 *ibid., p. 169.*

> but you sing a song like
> the clinking of schooners
>
> the city's still hearing
> when they're dead and gone.[10]

It's sweetly brutal, and its finality is lament as well as statement.

In 1995, Tracy and I attended the Melbourne Writers' Festival, staying on John Forbes's couch. I interviewed John. It was a bad night—it wasn't long after my giving up drugs and alcohol, and John was plastered. The interview itself is revealing but one that John later regretted. I am tempted to reproduce it, but as he decided against allowing its publication in life, I've decided to leave it in the archives. Still, here's a snippet that wouldn't offend him, and probably shows a little of the nature of our badinage:

Do you see this interview as a valid thing to do?

Yes, I suppose so. It's not something that ever occurred to me to do myself. I'm not attacking you doing it!

I'm quite used to being attacked by you ...

I don't attack you much.

Well, what did you call me this morning—it varied from paranoid, mad, horrible to despicable person!

When was this? I don't remember saying this. This morning? I was only joking. But you are a bit

10 *ibid., p. 171–3.*

*paranoid. I don't mean that as an insult. It probably
comes from sleep deprivation. You should sleep more,
learn to meditate or something. You are paranoid.
You tend to overreact to things.*

It's really interesting to note that poets for whom
drugs are a regular topic of conversation and in whose
poems drugs occur regularly, all, to a tee, deny that
they have any relevance whatsoever. You'll say, 'No,
it's totally irrelevant.'

Drugs? There are a lot of drugs in my poems.

But you say that they're irrelevant.

*Someone who's lived in the bush for three months and
is completely drug-free … they're a different sort of
poet. No, obviously, drugs are relevant to the poetry
of John Forbes.*

You need never have taken any to write what you've
written about drugs. They're totally irrelevant to the
textual thing.

*They put [American poet] Robert Lowell on lithium
and he never wrote a good poem again. But he
behaved a lot better.*

We talked a little about the work of the poet Peter
Porter, who now lives in England. John deeply admired
Peter Porter's wit and formal control over his poetry—his
dryness, his apparent confidence. Peter, like John, is not an
overly confident man, though: and maybe each knew this

of the other. Porter was a mentor figure: that's the way it worked. The maleness of it mattered to John. Plus Peter had gone to London: in John's mind not to betray Australia, but to show the Poms that Australians could do it better! The accusations of 'cultural cringe' made against those who left Australia in the 1950s and 60s to find a more cultural life in London were of course current in John's thinking, but Peter was such a great poet that he'd turned it against the centre. John was never blind to the battle of pushing poetry in Australia, and it made him despair at times, but he also believed that it didn't need to answer to elsewhere. In a speech I gave at the Melbourne Festival that time Tracy and I were staying with John, I discussed the need to be internationalist, for Australian poets to look outwards. He yelled out from the back of the audience something to the effect of 'Who cares what they think?'—basically, that we didn't need them. Jingoistic would be too simple a way of seeing it; it was more like not bending to 'their' will.

We had an e-mail message from John in Melbourne just before his death, saying with excitement that he'd got funding to come back to Cambridge. When we heard early the next morning, British time, that he had died, the message was still sitting there, unanswered.

7

Harold Bloom: a phone call

IT'S A BIT LIKE A GAME, answering this question: How did you meet Harold Bloom? It's one of my Amazing Stories, but one I don't think is ever really believed.

We were living in a very small flat in Como, Perth, Western Australia, not far from the Swan River, and with an insane tenant overhead who slammed dumbbells and phone books onto the floor to prevent us sleeping. Not that I did a lot of that. The phone rang at 2 o'clock in the morning and Tracy answered. She'd been working on her French translations that day, Katherine had been making chaos in her bedroom, and I'd been completing the poems that made up *Erratum/Frame(d)*. Tracy woke me:

You won't believe who is on the phone.

Who?

Harold Bloom.
Silence.

Ringing from New Haven.
Silence.

Are you going to take it?
Hi. It's John Kinsella speaking.

*Hello Mr Kinsella, it's Harold Bloom here. I hope you
don't mind my calling you like this, but a mutual
friend gave me your book* The Silo *to read and I felt I
needed to find you straight away.*

Harold went on to speak about the book. He deployed
his familiar terms of affection—'John, dear' and 'good
fellow'—and generally made me feel part of something. I
had spent a year coming off hard drugs, with great difficulty, and retreated to the Cocos Islands. I ended up in
trouble there (including being detained off a plane on
Christmas Island by federal police, for extreme inebriation
and making bizarre political statements), before returning
to WA, reconnecting with Tracy and deciding to give it
another go. Harold's message was—to be frank about it—
manna. And it came from heaven.

On a personal level, my entire family would benefit
greatly from the generosity and genuine caring of both
Harold and his wife Jeanne. There's no doubt Harold is a
complex character, and there are many different views of the
many different sides of him, but few doubt his generosity.

In person, Harold enjoys the theatrics of public interaction. A life of performing and a life of reading and watching performances of his beloved Shakespeare have meant Harold's actions have taken on some of the characteristics of the stage in general, but especially some of Shakespeare's characters. If Hamlet is the defining character for Bloom, and even pivotal to his belief that Shakespeare invented the Western notion of what it is to be human—a character who 'overhears himself' and consequently effects change in himself—then it is Falstaff, with his awareness of life's folly, with whom Harold associates himself personally. He has been quoted as saying that Falstaff is worth 'going over the top about' and that we find explications of 'personality' in this outsized figure of apparent jollity, mockery and parody. As Harold writes in *Shakespeare: The Invention of the Human*:

> Falstaff is anything but an elegiac figure; he would be fully present to consciousness, if only we could summon up a consciousness in ourselves to receive his. It is the comprehensiveness of Falstaff's consciousness that puts him beyond us, not in Hamlet's way of transcendence but in Falstaff's way of immanence.[11]

In person, Harold is large, but not like Falstaff, I feel, in either demeanour or deportment. In becoming the great literature he admires, he has become more himself, and more in touch with the working-class roots of the Bronx he in

11 *Harold Bloom*, Shakespeare: The Invention of the Human, *Fourth Estate, London, 1999, pp. 278–9.*

many ways left behind—the more secular Bloom, the more spiritual, to my mind. If there is a physical and psychological similarity, it's in Harold's observation that Falstaff has an 'extravagantly positive' exuberance. In so many senses of the expression, this is what attracts one to Harold. In his loves and hates, he is intense. Harold would like to see himself as 'never a hypocrite and rarely ambivalent', as he puts it. He would rather have the sins of the human than be the cardboard cut-out from academia that seeks to appease 'politically correct' notions in a time of aesthetic decline.

He has a warmth and affection that invite you into a hug, an embrace. His health has suffered over the years, and he will often discuss his mortality, then move rapidly on to a literary subject. His wispy white hair, still intensely curled, gives him a boyish appearance, despite his age. He will always self-reference and joke about his own celebrity, and his role in a conversation. I heard him introduce another eminent American critic to a friend recently in New York, at a reading in memory of his friend Archie Ammons, the poet, and he said that here was the greatest critic in America, to which he himself came a distant second. It was a complex rhetorical device: both ironising himself and also asserting his stature.

Harold is under no misapprehensions about his role in a room, in a university, among a reading public. He has dedicated his life to the art of reading and sees it as his mission to instil this love in others, to create a respect for great works. In the same way that he believes great poets rely on previous great poets, proving their own worth by (in a sense) out-writing those who came before, there is something of this in him as critic. One might look to Dr Johnson, or Emerson, or Northrop Frye, or even to creative writers for whom theory was an integral part of textuality, such as Shakespeare, a writer of 'meta-on-meta' texts. I believe Harold's struggle is with Shakespeare himself—and that is his rivalry.

I saw Harold reading extracts from *Henry IV*, part 2, on stage in New York. He played Falstaff with love, and spoke of Falstaff as himself: a figure of supposed ambiguity but, in reality, one without ambiguity at all. One could feel the love of literature that took Harold to Hart Crane as a young man, the love of language that took him to the Hebrew of his forebears as well as the Yiddish of his household, then American English (New York), then English of the early literary canon. A secular Jew, he has nonetheless valued his spiritual inheritance and is a unique critic in his comfort with hybridising Judaism and Christianity in his literary analyses. Bloom's fascination with the Yahweh 'author' (the J writer) is radically appealing to me. That the early texts of the Hebrew Bible (from the Pentateuch) are not only written by a literary figure—a writer—but that she is very likely a woman living in the court of King Solomon, I find an extremely liberating idea. And Bloom's engagement with the Gnostic found a template at home in my mother's fascination with gnosticism as an alternative route to vision and understanding.

Sitting together in New Haven (it suddenly strikes me that I have never seen Harold eating or drinking, as with

Fritz and Paul Bereyter in Sebald's *The Emigrants*), Harold told me that he'd just re-read *Paradise Lost* and that its majesty and spirituality were enhanced by the 'humanness', or maybe human failings, of Milton. Non-godlike status is no hindrance, and texts become more sublime for him, more terrible in their subtlety, by the fact of their humanity. The sublime is not only what nature can vastly or micro-cosmically present to us, to awe us; it is what can come of the human despite all failings and flaws.

During that same visit, Harold introduced me to the work of the black American poet Jay Wright and a number of first-volume poets I'd not come across. His comments on all of these contradicted what one is told to expect. Harold had been working very early in the morning—going to sleep around eight at night and getting up around four in the morning—and was in overdrive on the notions of genius (he was working on the Genius book). His assistant would come around in the morning and type the material he'd worked on before dawn. When Harold's wife Jeanne drove me to the station I told her how much my daughter had enjoyed his anthology of literature for 'bright children'. She told me how he never wanted to patronise children, as they could read with the best of them. And that's certainly been my experience. She spoke of her contempt for the view that reading a Stephen King novel once a year meant children had encountered and satisfied a need for great literature. For Jeanne, also, it's about reading the canon, and a lot of it. I share Harold's complete scepticism when it comes to Harry Potter …

Back to the issue of resentment. As someone sympathetic to multiculturalism (though not as government policy that in essence recognises difference in order to control and homogenise it), to feminism, black literatures, gay and lesbian literatures, deconstruction (of which Harold was once, somewhat erroneously, seen to be the 'father' in the United States), and so on, I find it annoying to be constantly told that my 'belief' in Bloomian thought is a contradiction. Well, as Walt Whitman said, 'Do I contradict myself? Very well, then, I contradict myself'. But it's actually more straightforward than that. Leaving aside Harold's gestures and sound bites of the moment, caught in an interview or a rhetorical (or dramatic) moment on stage—where he is, like most historically great critics, a performer—the essence of what he claims is that those who wish to deny aesthetic value are falsely trying to turn literature into politics/sociology, whereas the aesthetic is a crucially separate domain.

Maybe Joseph Conrad *was* a racist imperialist, but that does not mean he is not telling us something, that the text can't illuminate us against racism and imperialism. Literature is not instruction; it allows the reader to participate, interpret, and elevate above the words themselves. The issue is *how to read* Conrad. Reading Conrad does not mean we come away, necessarily, believing in racist and imperialist values; maybe the opposite. Two of Bloom's favourite poets, Whitman and Crane, were homosexual, but for him this doesn't define a separate poetics. It may be part of it, but what's primary is the aesthetic realm.

As the poet contests earlier poetry, as the poet tests him- or herself against the greats, progress comes of the rivalry. Judaism and Christianity can be in positive rivalry (as can other religions). Great literature comes of the struggle as well as spirituality. Whether through any of the categories Bloom has created: misprision (deliberate misreading) or, say, swerve (moving off in another direction), the engagement with predecessors, and what we most admire, is framed by an Oedipal struggle that propels us forward. Neither creating literature nor reading it is ever static for Bloom. I re-read *The Anxiety of Influence* in a hotel in Kansas City and it still struck me as relevant a decade after I'd first read it. I read *A Map of Misreading* in the wheat paddocks of York, Western Australia, and the same was true. What I ended up with both times was a sense that so many of Bloom's critics have recast what he'd already said, but through applying it to models outside his sense of canonicity. And I have done that myself: the anxieties and misreadings are done in local environments and circumstances as well: there are many smaller, regional (and significantly culturally separate or different) contexts in which the same actions are played out. Bloom's theories are not complete in themselves, and they can be applied where he might say it is less rewarding to go, but that's what theory is, to my mind: a starting point for the reader, not a set of instructions to a fait accompli. The same applies to his masterwork, *The Western Canon*. Try applying it as a template to 'Eastern literature', or maybe even local 'gay literature': though it seems a total contradiction, methodology and approach can yield interesting ideas about influence, hierarchy, reading, pleasure and 'value'.

In the late 1990s Harold visited Cambridge to discuss his *Shakespeare: Inventing the Human*. I went along to hear him—his old friend, critic Sir Frank Kermode, introduced him. Harold hadn't been feeling well, and his friends and colleagues kept close to him, by way of support. The reading and discussion were a great success, but the aura of celebrity inevitably leads to assumptions about access and favour. At question time a woman I didn't know (but would later know through Tracy) went up to ask Harold a question. She wanted his sole attention, clearly, but the crowd was large and a long line was behind her. She resented the acolytes gathering at Harold's heels (she told me one day long afterwards). She hadn't realised I'd been one of the 'acolytes' standing with him, and had noted her frustration at being given little time for conversation. Harold spoke with her a bit, then politely indicated that he had to speak with the next person. She took her annoyance, unfairly I felt, away with her. This is quite typical of book readings, but shows the difficulty of the public interaction that the 'reader' always expects to be a continuance of the private moment of the text. I am not sure if Harold would think this a bad thing.

The public's notion of what the eminent Yale professor should be is at odds with who Harold is. I originally found Bloom-the-critic through my interest in Hart Crane, and also Blake, Shelley and Wordsworth. His challenge to TS Eliot's reductive Christianising was especially welcome to a young poet trying to ignite nature and the prophetic. But his academic observations also went hand in hand with a breadth of reading that has defined my own life. You can sit and talk books endlessly with him. As a poet, he makes you feel connected with lines of poetic inheritance and he admires your breaking away from them as well. And if he misreads you, he opens a new line of thought, a new struggle with what it is you think you have written. When Harold says 'I prophesy', which he does when he is taken with something new, he does so with the moral conviction that he finds in the work of Shakespeare. The 'pronouncement' is intended not only to please but to stimulate action (on the poet's part: to be caught in the critical impetus). Criticisms of Bloom often overlook the real intention: to make things happen. To make the poet write more intensely, with a thirst for the Oedipal. And to make the reader take risks, work harder to gain the more 'sublime' of 'pleasures', and to create a greater kind of 'self'—i.e. to improve us, make us the best we can be. For all the intricacy (mimetic and semiotic) of Bloomian thought in the various stages (some say there have been three or four of these since the 1940s) of his literary, religious and cultural explorations, his principles are very clearly stated: literature is generative and enriching.

I have always gone looking for Harold since that phone call—as he has often said to me, Australia must remain a country of the mind for him, a distant place he can't reach because even short-haul flights destroy him. The Australia I have created in my poetry is an Australia of Whitman and Crane as much as of the poets Slessor and Wright. And Harold sees that. He has seen it's a vision in language as well as place.

It's about the vision, about the pleasure, and about the trouble of it all. In the end, Harold believes it brings reward, and that's the hope in a violent and destructive world. The night I heard him playing Falstaff to a full theatre in New York, he released a bitter diatribe against George W Bush and the death sentence. I admired him for that a great deal. Bloom's work affirms life, and at the top of the affirmation is a place for the Parnassian—the poet.

A few years after the initial phone contact, when I was visiting Harold and Jeanne in New York in the company of my literary agent (I'd acquired one—or was found by one—by then), who was very keen to meet him as well, I heard Harold being equally generous to a friend of his—a young woman, translator and academic, who, it would turn out, had brain cancer. At his request, I wrote a poem for her (I had liked her a lot on the evening I talked with her), and it is included in my *New and Selected Poems*, which Harold chose and introduced.

8

'Mr Sharpie'

JH PRYNNE'S ROOMS in Gonville and Caius College, Cambridge University, are split across two floors. Upstairs—right at the top—is his inner sanctum. We'll visit there later. Downstairs is his main office—a large desk, chairs, books, space for student gatherings during which students drink wine by the crate—provided by JH (Jeremy), but which he himself doesn't drink. Which doesn't mean he's a 'straight guy'—he's been places and seen things. But he is the perfect host—glasses are always filled, and conversation—radical conversation—is encouraged.

These soirées generate political and literary actions. Jeremy is now retired from university teaching, but over many years his lectures on the romantics and modern American poetry were as resonant and talked about as were

Wittgenstein's—students taking notes that became the fleshing-out of a life's philosophy. He feels at home with the young and enjoys their company. His vibrant mental and physical energy is that of a person in his twenties. On the wall opposite his desk is a painting by Peter Cartwright, a friend. Below this, on the floor, are piles of letters and packages, some opened, but most not, all awaiting their chance to be put into some order. It is rare to get a response from Jeremy Prynne, unless you have a close connection with him or spark his interest—and then the correspondence is dense, dedicated and immaculate. When I first visited that room, I wondered if any of the letters I had sent him over the years remained unopened among those piles.

The poetry of JH Prynne lured me to Cambridge. It is the story of fifteen years of my life. It came long before meeting him, but not before the idea of him. And this poet who has worked so hard to keep out of the limelight, or from 'prancing', as he would put it, became even more a figure of fascination. His poetry seemed to come out of his removal, his isolation, his denial.

In time I would learn this was not the case and that this great late modernist was great because of a lyrical verve that is melded with a scholarly capacity rarely seen in contemporary poetry. He took the lessons of the Black Mountain poets and Ed Dorn and others in the rushes of a new modernity in American poetry after the Second World War and applied it to the archives of his beloved Gonville and Caius College library, the University Library and basically all learning. Peter Porter once told me that, when he was in

Cambridge years back and 'Mr Prynne' (as he is known in Cambridge) rode past characteristically on his bicycle, a friend pointed and said 'There goes the smartest man in Cambridge.' So removed from the spotlight, and yet so fanatically dedicated to his students; it is also said, quietly, that the country would not function at all if you removed Mr Prynne's students from within its borders because they occupy so many positions of authority and power. When a review of his *Poems* was published in *The Guardian* a few years back, it was accompanied by a drawing of his well-known corduroy jacket and tie—that was all. He eschews being photographed, though some photos of him do exist. John Tranter has taken a few and placed one on the internet site of *Jacket* a long while ago; it was removed within days.

Speaking of the rhythms of writing, Mr Prynne rides his bicycle home to Ferry Path on the River Cam, *fast*, and given the length of time poems take to gestate, formulate and be written, then be published (most often in small-press publications or, for Jeremy, ones he has seen to print himself in order to get things right), it doesn't seem to be the place in which he thinks over his poetry. He does famously sleep during the day as much as possible and work through the night. There are many stories of students prostrating themselves outside his college window to howl at the moon *and* Mr Prynne, but these are (though often factual) part of a legend others have created around him.

There's another Prynne (or a number of Prynnes) and I feel, as an outsider, that I (along with Tracy) have had the privilege of experiencing this, and enjoying his friendship. Some have said it's because I am from outside Britain, that the rules are different. And that might be true.

We stayed at the Prynnes' for a couple of weeks late in 1996—well, I stayed a few days and left for the United States on a reading tour, and Tracy and Katherine stayed on as we were waiting for our new flat at Churchill College to become available. Katherine was just five years old. She was finding it hard to settle and (even then) of a flighty disposition but Jeremy found a sure-fire way of distracting and entertaining her. He'd often spoken about his daughters to me, but it became apparent that his fondness for children of whatever age was at the core of his personality. Gathering up a bunch of pencils, he started sharpening them in a desk sharpener. When each sharpened pencil emerged from the slot, Jeremy said to Katherine, 'Here's Mr Sharpie come to say hello to you, Katherine …' She loved it, and they went on whittling a variety of pencils into limbo.

Occasional moments, such as a brief comment by Jeremy on something as seemingly mundane as clearing out the garden shed or a realisation that the brand name imprinted on some item was a key to unravelling a clause in a Prynne poem, made time expand for me. As did opening a copy of a Wordsworth *Poems* on the bookshelves and finding marginalia by Jeremy giving a strange glimpse into the hermetic world of his subterranean lyricism. Jeremy's is not a post- or an anti- or any other stock epithet post-modern prefix of convenience; it is a lifelong investigation of what marks the song, makes love and elegy and material fact interweave in a poem. Its cryptics are not (only) to puzzle the reader, but to get somewhere, to see how far beneath what we perceive he might explore.

Suze, his retired physiotherapist wife, spoke in amused respectful whispers of Jeremy's work and his working methods. I have heard people conjecture many times on what it would be like to live with someone who works all night, but their lives have adapted to each other's, and Suze's own work is far from incompatible with Jeremy's own lifestyle. It's a remarkable relationship, and not mine to discuss, but their house is homely and inviting—not the place of the scholar, but the place of father and husband, mother and wife. Jeremy's wilder side is not felt there, one senses. Wilder side? Yes, he has one, and a fierce temper, but not, one feels, on Ferry Path.

With his hank of silver-grey hair hanging over a substantial forehead, and his immense though lightly fleshed frame, Jeremy cuts an impressive and memorable figure. Like most men of his generation, he has a history, I am told, of serving in the National Service army, or the equivalent of the Australian Nashos. His strong left-wing beliefs—his interest in and respect for Maoist China, and his resistance to conservatism in any form, are counterpointed by his collegiate life, the ritual of High Table (where he is his own man, no doubt), and university existence in general.

I can say that, when he comes back from his rooms in college in the morning, he reads *The Times*, which Suze may have read beforehand. Neither of them is conventionally religious or would line up with dogmatic beliefs. Ritual, however, is of interest to Jeremy. And the shape of his poems reflects this. The minutiae of observation are templated against the shafted windows of King's College Chapel, or against a field just outside town, and against form moulded over centuries in various languages.

French is an important language to Jeremy, and the first piece of his that I published in *Salt* magazine was actually the French translation of 'Day Light Songs' by Bernard Dubourg, a brilliant French poet and translator who Jeremy feels has been neglected and was harried by officialdom to an early death.

If Jeremy believes in you, it is entirely so. His striding gait marks time with yours, he looks down with intent (as most are shorter than him, though he and I are about the same height—maybe I am a little taller). He will befriend someone younger and shepherd them—he's fundamentally (I use this carefully) pastoral. Students seriously worship him. However, if you betray or are dishonest or set yourself up as something you are not, the condemnations are vituperative. He sees fraud everywhere, probably with validity. In some cases he judges harshly without explanation—I have heard him call particular public figures frauds, but not been sure why. He would have an argument to defend his point of view, though he might not offer it up for scrutiny if he didn't consider the occasion or company warranted it.

Mr Sharpie brings to mind a bizarre story. Over the years I have corresponded about encryptions in Prynne's work with Candice Ward, ex-managing editor of the *South*

Atlantic Review from Duke University. She was obsessively fascinated with Prynne's work and believed she had unearthed conspiracies in it against me. I made a joke to her that the truth lies in the sharpening of pencils, and that Mr Sharpie is really Jeremy's alter ego. I didn't offer much explanation. In essence it came to pass that, when referring to the Tristram Shandyisms, Rowleyisms (my guess), alchemical, rune-isms, and medievalisms in Prynne's work, JHP is entitled Mr Sharpie. It's a witticism that parries and thrusts in all sorts of directions.

Yenyenning

The Australian landscapes are a long way from the interior landscapes of Prynne's poetry and his scholarship. Or are they? Prynne's close friendship and extensive correspondence with poets Charles Olson and Ed Dorn meant a contact not only with the innovations of post-Second World War American poetry but also with 'new' and physically expansive histories. These poets and Prynne himself had to deal with a page that simply couldn't hold enough. Prynne's poetry is so contained by and attached to the page that it might seem at odds to make the claim. But in its way it is expansive, folding in on itself, creating a topology of its own. Language is landscape, ideas are place.

JH Prynne visited Australia as a guest of the Landscape and Language Centre at Edith Cowan University in August 2002. As mentioned earlier, Jeremy avoids public contact or public scrutiny. But his *Poems* had just been jointly published by Fremantle Arts Centre Press, *Salt*, and Bloodaxe Books, and he felt it important to support the publication with his presence in a way he'd never do back in England. Away, in different co-ordinates, he could behave differently. In some ways, he is 'quintessentially' English, as they say, but he relishes the chance to depose the structures of class and national expectation. His sympathies with Maoist China come about from a belief that different 'systems' suit different places, and he despises the arrogance of those who try to impose the politics of their place on another—he sees this as culturally insensitive, offensive, and foolish. Jeremy's connection with China goes back a long way, and he has stood by groups of Chinese poets so strongly that he has cut connection with publishers because of their unwillingness to publish innovative Chinese poets in translation though wanting his own work. Bloodaxe fell into this category, and only through my persuading him that it would be best for the book to have that more 'out-there' connection did he go with them. It should be clarified that supporting a Maoist Chinese government doesn't mean he supports the oppression of artists, poets and individuals in general, but that he feels Westerners should keep their noses out of what they don't understand.

Jeremy's main interest in visiting Australia was to explore the Kimberley region. I went to his rooms at Gonville and Caius College once or twice when he had maps out and was pointing out where he'd like to go. He was fascinated by indigenous Australia, and it seemed to him that was where he might make some form of contact. Jeremy's reactions and observations are 'recorded' (not that easy) in the poem he wrote in response to his visit to Australia; his dismay at the racism and bigotry towards, and lack of appreciation of, the indigenous peoples of those regions is heart-felt. Not long after his arrival in WA he saw the film *Rabbit-Proof Fence* and commented on what he felt was the simplicity and polarisation of the message of the film: black/good, white/ bad. I think after his journey he might have seen it a little more like that, but I am guessing and reading into the poetry. These are three stanzas of Jeremy's *Acrylic Tips*, primarily written out of experiences of his stay:

> Called down, each night over to dawn falling out ahead:
> woven door traps, long and thin. Unmelted sugar pan
> venerated lodge, lesson throat veins. Intimated product
> recall goes out overland toiled back and descending

> In bright glance, yielding credence ridden to limit store
> hacking swift pine and juniper, grubbing roots. Doing
> all turns, invert sweetness at the curtain grassy open
> plain payment due. The way chanted and bound up

> Most to let nothing fall, not coming back to back sounds
> fluent spill sealant entrance drupe, thrown by high
> winds made away no word from either stitching a breath
> let flow, pipes to ground glass to unslaked level fields.[12]

For someone who eschewed publicity, it must have been a shock for him to deal with stuff like this from the univer- sity news: 'Poet Shares Trade Secrets', including a photo of

12 *from JH Prynne,* Poems, *2nd edn,* Bloodaxe Books *&* Fremantle Arts Centre Press, *Fremantle, WA, 2005, p. 546.*

Jeremy holding his book. It must have hurt, but with good grace he endured.

Jeremy also wanted to come to Australia because Ian Friend, an artist with an interest in his work, had moved there in 1985 and shown some of his Prynne-inspired work in an exhibition at the National Gallery of Australia in 2004, although 'the vast expanses of central Australia' frustrated hopes to meet in person.

Poets from John Forbes to John Tranter and Gig Ryan were aware of Prynne's work, and some were ardent admirers, especially Tranter, who had struck up a friendship with Jeremy in Cambridge at an earlier date and stayed as his guest in Gonville and Caius College. Prynne's linguistic work didn't compare with any Australian poetry (other than, maybe, in language displacement, the work of Lionel Fogarty, the Murri poet), but it offered an alternative to the academy-led and (by now) doctrinaire Language poetry from the United States.

Jeremy was staying at the Inglewood Hotel, and though it was a rough working pub, with a hardcore bikie and drug clientele (I know from the old days when I lived in Bedford and used to drink there—it was all speed and Harleys; no dreadlocks, which I had at the time), Jeremy fitted in well there, and was tolerant, even respectful, of the noise. The well-mannered, be-suited don of Gonville and Caius College is no shrinking violet. He knows an orange tie might be a little too much for them in the front bar, so it's open collar. He gets on well with the barmaids: I see him banter with them early in the morning when they're setting up for the day's drinking. They like him, and years of teaching postgraduate women of the same age gives him an indulgent respect which goes down so well in these parts.

Jeremy was having trouble with his 'ancient' laptop, and we agreed that he would ring England when he got to our place—for the long-promised stay in York—to see what he should do regarding a spare part for it. A few days earlier (or was it later?), I had taken him to Fremantle (the port) to a computer dealer who repaired old machines. He couldn't get the part necessary for Jeremy's machine, so he had to call England to sort it out. Jeremy insisted on retaining the old technology.

We picked him up in the old red Falcon Fairmont—huge motor and huge body to sail the country roads. Pickup like a drag car, lots of torque. He liked it. On arriving at our place, he greeted my mother and brother, all of us living in separate parts of the large multi-sectioned house. Two aspects of Jeremy's visit stand out for me. One was the bond he made with my brother, who was nearing the end of his 'out-of-it' period and wasn't in a good way; the other was our trip together out to Yenyenning.

My brother Stephen, the shearer, was an angry man with a refusal to accept the mythology of his world, kicking against the pricks at every chance. He'd been treated harshly by pretty well everyone and was as rebarbative as they come. Steeped in Stephen's music—pathological guitar, drums, and didgeridoo—the spare room in Stephen's end of the house was set up for Jeremy. Neither had the habit of sleeping at night, so both spent the evenings talking, and discussing many things that only they will know and Jeremy's poetry will not reveal. This special friendship then seemed to go underground or I lost sight of it, after they parted, which is not to say that a responsive thread is still not there. I have one visual memory of their interaction: Jeremy leaning up against the wall while Stephen played didgeridoo—Jeremy seemed to be staring into himself like someone undergoing a shamanistic drug ritual, a door of perception that had opened ironically and had then gone to some place without language or name. As in his poems. There was a non-understanding understanding in it all, both ways.

Jeremy woke to a breakfast cooked by Mum, some piano (Mum would record a CD of her own classical compositions not long after Jeremy's visit), and a clearish winter's day. The southwestern Australian winter was hot enough for Jeremy, though he'd handle the extreme heat of the Kimberley later. He didn't complain.

We drove out to Yenyenning late in the morning, along the Great Southern Highway, taking the gravel road turn-off to Yenyenning and County Peak. I told him the history of Walwalinj, the 1300 foot hill out the back of our place that had been 'discovered' by Ensign Dale and crowned the glory of the eroded Dyott Range (named after a general, with Walwalinj being called Mount Bakewell after a mate of Dale's). I told him how once two young lovers, who had been forbidden by their tribes to be together, eloped and were caught, with the punishment of being turned into mountains or hills at opposite sides of the river valley—the large mountain being Walwalinj, the young warrior male;

and the smaller hill Wongborel, the young woman from the neighbouring tribe. The story goes that they will not see each other again until the two hills come together. Jeremy found it fascinating that York is near a major faultline, and that it's possible that an earthquake *will* bring them together one day.

We drove through the florescent green paddocks—the wheat in full growth at that time—past the wandoos, jam trees and York gums (the gnarled and flat-coloured plants draw obvious contrasts to Europeans; I can never get bored with them). We took the gravel, and the old Ford rode it at a hundred plus with barely a bump, where a newer, more streamlined car would have been fishtailing and losing control. I explained about the vast patches of salinity that we passed, the different species of birds that made a go of them. Jeremy has only ever referred directly to my poetry three times in all the years I have known him: once when I asked permission to dedicate something to him; another time when he talked about Australian poets in general; and on this occasion when he said he could really see my poetry here. That mattered to me, and there's nothing else to be got out of it.

When we turned onto the road to the Yenyenning Lakes (though it could have been returning on the same spur road), twenty-eight parrots started doing their long, loping undulations alongside the car. It's one of their characteristics to locals: they race vehicles, or seem to. I said to Jeremy: 'as kids we used to drag twenty-eights on the motorbike ...' He seemed momentarily shocked, as if it didn't compute with all the animal rights stuff and veganism. 'That sounds excessively cruel ...' he responded. It took a second, then I laughed in my paranoid way: 'No, no ... I mean we drag-*raced* them on the motorbike ...' But, in a sense, he was still close to being right: my veganism comes out of my later disgust with shooting hundreds of these beautiful birds for the sport of it when I was a kid.

Yenyenning Lakes is one of the most notorious eco-disasters of the region. Originally a series of lakes that fed into the Avon River, they have been turned excessively saline and basically destroyed by mismanagement and outright abuse. The local 'Beverley Ski Club' (still going) dammed off the lakes so they would hold water all year round—inland water-skiing. When combined with excessive land clearing and the consequent leaching of salt out of the soil because of a rising water table, the run-off of farm nutrients, and the interference with natural flood regimes, the salinity in the lakes became so toxic that most of the surrounding vegetation perished. If you look at them now, you see hectares, even miles, of dead trees puncturing the sky like broken bone. It's a sick sight. It's now a place of hoons: of illegal duck-shooting (the lakes, which spread out like Ian Friend's painting of Jeremy's 'ovals' towards the South Avon River, are actually a nature reserve now)—shotgun cartridges littering the swampy banks and bulldozed sand drifts, drunken barbecues and speedboating, and fear. There is still 'Nature' there, and you'll often see mulga parrots and many other birds in abundance, but the strain is increasing rather than decreasing. Efforts at preservation are met with more condoned vandalism.

So to the eye of the storm I took Jeremy.

We headed down a sand track and parked the car. It fascinated him; we were the only people there. He removed a small fold-up magnifying glass from his pocket and started examining the trunks and remnant bark of dead trees, saying 'Hmmm, hmmm, I see ... yes, yes, I see ...' He did this intently for ten minutes, then did the same with a living tree. I could see notes of comparison being taken in his head. He was still in his semi-formal dress, though his demeanour seemed more relaxed than usual. Jeremy has a slight lisp; there, it went entirely. We explored a small area of the reserve closely, like working on a single stanza rather than a whole poem. I showed him a massive female red-back spider that had built its web over the shadowy entrance of an abandoned (or trapped, or shot, or poisoned-out) rabbit warren—I'd seen it a few weeks earlier when I'd visited with Tracy and Katherine. I saw a pair of elegant parrots and went traipsing after them, leaving Jeremy to his own devices. When I found him again, he was examining one of the thousands of small snail shells that line the shores of the lakes. My other memory is of how carefully he trod through the bush, his long legs pincering their way through the remnant vegetation. He gained my lifelong respect for this.

A few months ago, I took my children out to Yenyenning without thinking to tell anyone where I was heading. It was after heavy rain and the track (broken by two cattle grids) out to the lakes was partially under water. In a new Corolla (not the country-worthy Ford), I came to one large puddle on the edge of a stand of dead York and flooded gums. I thought it would be firm beneath, so started easing the car through. Within seconds the car was bogged to the axles and we were in deep trouble. Timmy was only two and a half, and Katherine was easily stressed out. But seeing the gravity of it, both kids remained calm. I got out into the mud, found the picnic blanket (plastic-lined) in the boot, lodged it under/behind one of the front wheels (front wheel drive), and asked Katherine to stand in the mud in front of the car and push. She did, I eased it back and then backed it out. Katherine and I were covered in mud, but we had shared a close call. It can get like that at Yenyenning, though it's probably less than thirty kilometres from the town of Beverley. The back road from Yenyenning takes you via County Peak, and this was the way I took Jeremy.

County Peak is a tormenting aberration. It is the local high point in that area. The lakes are very low, forming a basin, and County Peak surveys them. It is on private property, and as part of a civic gesture, the farmer has fenced it off to form a nature reserve and tourist attraction. His action is supported by the local council and other authorities. But during the last drought, I was distressed (even if I understand why) to see that he opened the fence and let sheep in to graze on the native vegetation. The place is a torment because it should be so important, yet it is so damaged. Clearing of the peak has led to massive erosion, with one side like ripped flesh. At the top there's an old asbestos dunny that's been knocked down (God knows why it was there; asbestos is broken and strewn everywhere), and a survey marker. But there's enough vegetation to get a sense of what it had been like.

Jeremy climbed one of the semi-eroded faces and stood at the summit, looking out. An eagle appeared distantly. It was a stilled moment in time. We didn't say much there, as at Yenyenning, though I did later write a poem about it with a small blue flower as the focal point. Jeremy, between silences, most often asked me the common and scientific names of things. He was especially interested in scratchings and dung identification, and in flowers. Near the summit of the peak, there was that single small blue flower. He thought he recognised it from an earlier excursion (maybe with Glen Phillips). It looked like a *Dampiera*, and I confirmed that I thought it was this. The isolated and bedraggled look of the flower, though, cast some doubt: normally there'd be a shrubby (small) bush with many flowers, but this was a single strand, a typical plea for life in impoverished conditions. Jeremy really wanted confirmation, but I felt I had to check to be sure. The naming seemed vital to him. Prynne is the most intellectual of poets: he dismantles the physical world through etymology, grammar, science, history and experience. There is a hermetic or sealed side to all of Jeremy's poetry. You can try to decode his poems, but in the end you will hit the gravel underneath, which was there for eons before the fabrications of the written and is much harder to penetrate. People call it difficult, but if you look simply rather than complexly, you'll see that it's almost pagan in its chanted rituals. Religion is a control that it rejects, but spiritual investigation is one it cherishes. Especially of friends, family and places.

Driving back home in the old Ford, I lost a hubcap as we went over one of the many corrugations in the road. I told Jeremy how the kids of one family's place we passed had tormented Mum at the country school where she'd previously been teaching. They hate teachers, and just want to get back to the farm; their resentment is at having to leave the farm. This is a land full of resentment and anger at loss, dispossession, ownership and rights. It is a conflicted place of erosions. Jeremy said he could see it was probably so.

It wasn't hard for Jeremy to see how colonising has fucked up much of the Australian landscape. Sure, it's not as simple as good and bad, but it is as simple as have and no longer have. I've asked Jeremy to come back, and he thinks he might.

My dream has nothing to do with poetry, academia, and the 'art.' It's just the way I've chosen to express myself. What I have to say is hard to express; I find it easier in poetry. A poet like Bob Adamson would be disgusted with this. I say 'believe in the poetry' to those *I* mentor, but I don't really believe it. I am, as Tracy said the other day, interested in family, place and ethics. I want to save areas of native bushland. I want to lock them away from exploitation, and I want to return them to indigenous peoples (who can exploit land as much as any, but have tens of thousands of years more experience at positive custodianship in the main).

Jeremy said he'd return to speak—publicly—at such a handing-over, if I achieved my aim. All those who know Jeremy outside Western Australia, where few in fact know him, would laugh that he'd come back to a place that produced such wisdoms as: 'Renowned British poet Jeremy H Prynne is sharing the secrets of his success with ECU students from now until early September.' But then, many have expressed annoyance that he allowed a bunch of Australians to look after the publication of his *Poems*, which, as he says, was done with such meticulous care. Yet that's the point—the whole point. Jeremy knows his work needs distance, as he does himself. That's his secret—or one of them.

9

Four photos at
Wordsworth's grave

WE DON'T HAVE a lot of photos of our years as a family in England, but there is a batch taken one day at Wordsworth's grave, with Michael Hulse, the renowned translator and poet, appearing in most of them, as Tracy and I alternately disappear from photos we take of each other. It's a cold day, and we're rugged up. Katherine is tiny—maybe five years old.

The focus of the photographs is not Wordsworth, nor his grave. The photos are poorly lit—it was a characteristically overcast Lakes day. Winter. A mixture of evergreens and deciduous trees, holding out what light there was. It's some years back, as I've got a blue windcheater on under my black denim jacket, and I stopped wearing anything other than black a long time ago. There are traces of grass on the ground; the mud overwhelms it. Drystone walls are green with lichen and moss. Iron fencing has been bolted into the top layers, encircling the graveyard. The wrought-ironwork around the graves is painted against rust.

Michael is dressed in a grey suit, with open-necked pink–red shirt. His hair is short, brown; his glasses are round. He is looking at the graves and I am looking at him. I have an awkward expression—a cross between grinning and reacting to glare. I am more 'rugged up' than Michael—who doesn't feel the cold much. I too am that way these days, after years of living in cold climates, but I wasn't then. We seem to visit graves and churches when we're 'on the road', and art galleries. But maybe in Europe that's what everyone visits. They are the markers of loss and memory. Michael is at home among them. He is the same in Germany.

Of both English and German parentage, Michael is a child of the Second World War insofar as his parents' relationship came about through a blending of the post-war worlds of the two countries. A crisis of identity—that has made him such a brilliant translator—has fed his Englishness; though bilingual, and having lived a vast amount of his adult life in Germany, he seems more English than German. He writes his poetry in English, and *is* English. His much-lauded translations of WG Sebald's prose work so well—though Sebald complained they were more Hulse than himself, at times—because of that displacement in geography (always one country or the other), but also sensibility.

In this Lake District graveyard I am reminded of the Harvill edition of WG Sebald's *The Emigrants*, beginning with the hazy black-and-white image of a graveyard ... And the description of a house in Michael's translation: 'One of the largest in the village, it stood a short distance from the church with its grassy graveyard, Scots pines and yews, up a quiet side street.' This is the house where 'Sebald' (the text's narrator) first lived in 1970 when he moved to take up his position at the University of East Anglia, Norwich. Michael is also a lover of such houses, though the ramshackleness might be less appealing.

The merging of descriptive precision, even lushness at times, and a bleak reality of loss, of destruction of culture, of isolation and loneliness, resonates through Sebald's *The Emigrants*, the first translation of Sebald that Michael gave us. He didn't inscribe the book, nor *The Rings of Saturn*, but his translation of *Vertigo* is inscribed: 'for dear Tracy on her birthday from her friend the translator—Michael 27 IX 1998'. I think of *The Emigrants* because of dislocation, and of the German Michael translates from and is part of, and the destruction of 'humanism' by the Holocaust. I think Michael would defend humanism to a degree, but the edges are bitter for him. Perhaps Michael's Catholicism does not allow the collective guilt of national identity to be removed—nation is how we define ourselves (I am local, not national, and internationally regional), but the crimes done in its name are not to be erased or hidden from. I believe this is Michael's crisis, and what I believe has attracted him so strongly to Sebald's work, especially regarding the crimes of Germany, a conflicting love of the German language, and a cultural dualism. Sebald left the 'old Germany' to move to England, and his analysis and conjecturing on place, history and culture are focussed through his coming out of, and being part of, something he deplored. Michael's movement is almost the opposite—his soldier father marrying the German woman after the end of the war, the revelation of the death camps, and the destructions of culture.

In Germany with Michael, it always amazed me how British he was—whether it was at the British Council in Cologne, or translating television programmes into German from English for the German TV network Deutsche Welle, or working on his German texts for English readers. A go-between, Michael generously linked Americans and Canadians and Australians and Brits (as well as others) within the 'foreignness' of the new Germany, always citing an awareness of two or more pasts: that of the Nazis (and how that came to be) and that of, say, Goethe. Though these elements are intellectually inseparable, Michael seems to have created his own dialogue of reconciliation with place by separating them off. Even if in many ways Michael is an anti-Romantic poet, it is his concept of a Romantic Germany that moves him to send us Christmas notes and e-mail regarding the beauty of the village, or even city, and even in Staffordshire, 'celebrating Christmas in the German way, on Christmas Eve, with dinner in Lichfield and midnight service in the cathedral to follow', for example. I often think Michael's general irreverence is a coping mechanism for a dislocation and anger that the wonder of language is not enough in itself to prevent horror. Maybe, being more English than German, Michael has an 'escape' from the weight of it all … but is drawn back knowing he is part of the efforts to heal what in truth can, for many, never be healed.

Back at Wordsworth's grave, I recall wondering how a poet who has written so much of death, and would write much more in the years to come, confronts his own mortality while always being conscious (as translator, poet and 'humanist') of his obligations in working with a language associated with a specific history of genocide. Michael is enigmatic that way and will turn a moment of seriousness aside with 'humour', always looking disturbed and guilty afterwards, even apologising.

Michael says, 'You know Wordsworth used to walk along and kick in molehills and the like …' Wordsworth as anti-nature poet? I think there's something in that, beneath Michael's irony. Recall Wordsworth's inscriptions poem where the persona meets the vicar out in the mountains, who is aghast at seeing that 'Wordsworth' has inscribed a woman's name on a stone—a vandalism of the nature he purports to love ('Poems on the Naming of Places').

Tracy reminded me of the way he took to the wheel on that visit. He drives fast and jerkily. There's a manic energy tossed in with anger and distraction. Michael has a lot of things to do at any given time, and they happen in the car. He will study a map on the steering wheel as he hurtles towards a branch in an M road. Tracy recalls how he teased Katherine about the lambs—'mint sauce', he quipped, but according to Tracy, Katherine didn't get the nasty joke, because of course, being raised vegan, she'd never heard of lamb with mint sauce. He talked about his father's stroke, loss of language, Tracy recalls.

On that same road trip we paid a visit to John Ruskin's grave and I remember the minor argument Michael and I had over it, or over Ruskin. Ruskin is—or was—one of Michael's heroes. And why wouldn't he be? One of Ruskin's early forays into art criticism was an unpublished essay defending Turner, and his later infatuation with pre-Raphaelitism fits perfectly Michael's occasional interest in images of the languorous, maudlin female.

Ruskin believed in the essential nature of imagination and the fantastic. I have always associated his notion of the grotesque with Michael's poetics and world view. It seems to be at the core of Michael's own aesthetics. Further to this, his desire to meld poetry, art, politics and society into a congruent 'high art' is certainly Ruskinesque in temperament, though Michael is more sympatico with Harold Bloom in his belief in good and bad writing.

Michael was actually very kindly towards Katherine. And as a way of apologising for his 'mint sauce' quip, he wrote her animal poems every birthday for some years. They still offended on the level of veganism and animal rights, but the irony was self-irony, and that can't hurt anyone. Language is a dynamic to Michael, and just because something seems to say one thing doesn't mean it can't say another.

Stand magazine has been one of Britain's major post-war literary journals which has published everyone from Jean-Paul Sartre to Wole Soyinka. Legendary in its own way, and certainly in its own mind or the mind of its founder and those close to him, Jon Silkin. Called *Stand* because it would 'stand alone', and maybe 'take a stand', it was seen by Silkin as Northern and working-class, with an internationalist flavour. A journal of the left, it suffered from a male-orientated contents list and tendency to the conventional (to my mind) in expression.

Michael Wilding had been the Australian editor for some years. When Michael Hulse and I took over the editorship, *Stand* was in decline from its apparent peak circulation of around 6000—enormous by British standards. We were told at this point by those who were looking after the magazine's affairs that circulation was at 5000—when in fact it was around 2800. What we then did with *Stand* created upset and controversy that still resonates years later. The good and bad of it came about from the tension and difference in Michael's and my editorial and design concerns. First, we changed the journal from its familiar landscape format into a larger portrait-format journal with colour cover. Even more internationalist, we also quadrupled payment to contributors and developed a thematic format. The *Stand* old guard saw it as becoming culturally elitist, though there were numerous strong gestures to a broader vision of the left than had appeared before. Whatever one's views, the outcome was a result of many conflicts, especially between my anarchist stance and Michael's individualist pragmatism. Tensions with the board of trustees, and the old guard's fear that we were taking the journal conceptually out of the North (and physically towards Cambridge), saw a bitter end to our time there.

Truth is, we would have moved it to Cambridge. Leeds University had a vested interest in this not happening. We did spend more money than we should have. The journal's board was caught between the journal and a desire to perpetuate the cult of Jon Silkin's memory (it was Silkin's death that had led to the search for new editors). Michael had got to calling the managing editor pet names, in response to what he saw as his lack of support for us, and wasn't surprised when they offered for me to stay on with the journal while Michael would be dropped. But we had gone in together, and we left together. The old guard wanted us as servants to Silkin's memory, whereas we saw the journal as ours for the editing. Anyway …

We'd been planning a Nobel Prize issue of *Stand* for some time. There's a story here. So, to a possible beginning. No, to *the* beginning: Churchill College and the visit of the eminent Swedish physicist Professor Svante Lindqvist. I came across Svante in the crucible that's the Senior Common Room. We got talking about his physics work and then my work—at that time, on *Salt* magazine. This led to the idea that maybe *Salt* could do an issue based on the Nobel prizes, to time with the opening of the Nobel Museum in Stockholm. It would be a free-ranging investigation—warts and all. I have major problems with prize culture, though I have always been happy to take a cheque if I've managed to score. Common paradox, I think. The Nobels are founded on industrialist—and specifically dynamite—money. That's a worry. But the idea was that we could explore all this, and celebrate the genuine creativities of many recipients. Over the ensuing year Svante and I swapped e-mails, and a project began taking shape. Other people such as Marika Hedin came into the picture.

When I first met Svante, I hadn't yet started at *Stand*. After responding to *Stand*'s advertisement for editors, and having talked it over with Michael, we had attended our interview in Leeds and started immediately. I mentioned the Nobel prospect to Michael and we agreed to do it as a *Stand* issue, instead of my doing it at *Salt*. It took two years to gestate and come together, by which stage *The Kenyon Review* had come on board. It was a massive project. In the end, the *Stand* old guard's opposition to the 'elitism' of this project was the final nail in our coffins.

As part of the growing project, Michael and I had to visit Sweden on three or four occasions to work with the Nobel Museum people. We'd formed a literary committee, and a number of advisers became involved. At the final meeting the editors of *The Kenyon Review* flew in from Ohio to join Michael and me at the final planning session. The irritation had begun at lunch when Michael and I argued over a child-ish 'who would deserve a Nobel more: Curnow or John Ashbery?' It was ridiculous, as I didn't really care and thought it irrelevant. For Michael, Ashbery was a non-starter, and the still-living Curnow was the greatest poet writing in English. I think the others at the table were bemused.

It's worth considering Michael's own highly successful poetry at this stage. In many ways, Michael was at the fore-front in Britain of writing poetry in syllabics—a form usually associated with French. It's not surprising, as his rhythms were those of two languages, and rather than obfuscating one with the other, he chose an orderly and measured approach to 'the line'. It suits his character—words in the right order.

Michael often looks America-wards, but in many ways the United States eludes him as a country and a culture. He is not sure how to bridge that gap, though his translations have been successful there. And translation is also where his syllabics come from—the setting up of a template to take the wider prosaic language of explication. His master-work is the collection *Eating Strawberries in the Necropolis*, in which 'art' and language are placed under the micro-scope of mathematical precision.

The most moving poem of Michael's is his poem in memory of his father—a poem that shifts between struc-tural rigour and (over) heightened emotional expression. He needs to hold himself back in case he starts to release more than he can control. He is a master of light verse. The prob-lem, though, with his ironic satirical poems is never their pace or balance but the occasional faux pas or moment of extreme bad taste. You'll never get him to stop—he relishes offended reactions too much. He is good at taking the piss out of those who read him with the 'PC' eye. We published his new and selected poems at Salt—*Empires and Holy*

Lands—a book in which he presents his own grand narratives, his own theories of culture and intra-culture. The poems roused one reviewer to a furious tirade against what he claimed was Michael's bigotry and offensive attitudes, especially to women. The accusation of misogyny, and worse, actually did manage to offend Michael, as it was a grotesque misreading of intent. When he has been hurt, his face reddens and his eyebrows lift, and he either explodes or completely withdraws into himself, shakes his head, lifts a book from his shoulder bag and replaces it, rocks on his heels, then leaves.

That book bag of his has led to many poets getting international audiences. Michael collects books and reads them. He will promote a poet simply on a reading, and his enthusiasm is boundless. He knows why he likes work, and is not easily rebuffed. Arguing over poets to publish at *Stand*, we often found we were pushing for the same poet with different views on what they were doing. I like disjunction, non-connection, a lack of closure—Michael prefers a crafted holism, a structured universe. In time, this changed too—whether it was circumstantial and the right work for him came along, or whether it happened because of our interaction, I don't know. I certainly learnt about European literary culture from him. The man is encyclopaedic in his knowledge.

Sweden. We are staying at the same hotel together—Michael, David Lynn, Tom B. and myself. I am close to

David, and I am fond of Tom B.—who will die of cancer not more than a year after this. A gentle, generous man, it was he who offered to drive me around when I first went to Kenyon College to do a reading. I spent an afternoon on his property before it was sold, walking the edges, and wrote a poem about it. A requiem. Tom B. was disturbed by what he felt was Michael being pretty harsh on me. It was a crisp April and as we walked to the museum for a meeting and then back Michael kept trying to catch me out with flaws in argument, or misquotes, and the like. He was annoyed about something. Stockholm is a city built on islands, and as you cross bridges from one to another, you have a sense of dislocation/connection, of exits and entries that can't be resolved. I like those bridges. A cutting wind blows over them as you emerge from buildings over the clear waters (they weren't always!)—it sharpened Michael even more. We had just left the oldest part of the city, and Michael was testing me. I wasn't interested and walked ahead with Tom. Michael spoke louder so I could hear him. It was about dinner that night, and how the vegan would be fed. Same old thing.

I first heard from Jon Silkin in 1997, not long before his death. He rang me at Cambridge to sound me out about *Stand*, which he felt needed a boost—he thought I might be able to help with this. The conversation trailed off into a discussion of his metrics book and about how he might get it reviewed. I am not sure what led him to ring me—it came out of the blue. I never met him in person, but would certainly come to know him indirectly.

Michael Hulse and I shared a vision of poetry: it should be culturally pluralistic, and should be made available to readers in times when publishers' lists were diminishing. We enjoyed publishing each other, and others. I didn't mention the Silkin call until *Stand*'s editorship was advertised. Michael contacted me and said we should try for this— we could shake up Brit poetry. An Englishman based in Germany and an Australian based in Cambridge.

Offered an interview in Newcastle, we went by rental car and discussed all the way there how we would approach it. Michael is methodical, and had prepared notes and outlines. We had a literary track record between us, and both of us have the gift of the gab, so sitting in front of the editorial board was not difficult. They liked our sell, they liked our plans for reinvigorating the magazine.

The journal itself had moved from its long-term association with Newcastle to Leeds. Silkin had sold the journal's archive (and his own papers) to Leeds University not long before his death. After his estate was settled, a large amount went into trust, financed by the *Stand* archive. The whole time we were at *Stand*, every document that passed through our hands, every note we scribbled, went into the Leeds Library collection, generating thousands of pounds a year in income for the journal, and the trust.

As Michael lived in Cologne, I tended to visit the office in Leeds more regularly than he did. We hired a PhD student, Helen, who in essence ran the office. She also contributed to the African issue and its editorial. She was a mainstay, though very conservative in managing things and constantly reminding us of the purse strings. I liked her a lot, but she frustrated Michael, especially with her poor grammar. I like bad grammar; sort of! Editorials were an issue for me—I primarily wrote two of them, a couple in conjunction with Michael, and he pretty well wrote the rest. I disagreed with the instructional nature of an editorial—themes were enough. I felt it straitjacketed things. These editorials further infuriated the old-time subscribers, so upset with the change to the portrait format.

Every two or three weeks I would make the journey by train from Cambridge. The journal (in theory) covered my travel and B & B near the university. If I came back on a Saturday, I occasionally paid for 'weekend first'—an extra ten pounds to travel first class. More space, more work done on the train. I found the commuting stressful, especially with train changes at Wakefield or Doncaster, sometimes Ely, but I got to know the run well, and for me it's more the scene of *Stand* magazine than Leeds itself. A burgeoning city, Leeds did fascinate me, but it also alienated me in the way big cities do. It's not that big in its centre, just sprawled *and* intense. If I was taking a break from the journal, I'd wander the short distance downtown. *Stand* was ensconced in its second storey of the English faculty offices—one room for files and fax and the like, another for editorial, with a further room at the top of the building which stored back issues of the journal. Those back issues existed in such large numbers from *Stand*'s fifty years (with the exception of early issues which are incredibly rare) that they also filled an entire shed.

The train journey up through the fens to Leeds might seem monotonous to some, but to me it was like journeying through the outback of Western Australia. It's different in so many ways but similar in its lack of 'relief'. A bird, or flock of birds, against its surfaces disrupts the sense of space. A small place looks immense. The sky connects with the soil at myriad points, not just on the horizon line—and this because it looks so far above it that your sight forces them together to cope.

On one or two occasions I went across to Todmorden to see the crew at Arc publishing, printer–publishers somewhat in the mode of the radical publishers working in Britain at the time of the French Revolution, with a special regard for poetry from around the world. The train goes through Bradford and across the Pennines—suppressed mountains. On the journey, I remember, a group of rugby players were extremely drunk and abusing Pakistani Brits—sign of things to come. It was outrageous, and the more so for it being tolerated by everyone else on the train.

Most often the Arc people would come across to Leeds to see me, and sometimes both Michael and me. After Michael left Arc, things were a little awkward, but friendships remained. Arc advertised in *Stand*, and we supported their books with reviews, as we did all the other British poetry publishers. We weren't worried about issues of favouritism because we reviewed what we liked from wherever. This was one great thing about working with Michael:

he didn't fear accusations of nepotism in any way. The literary world gets obsessed about these things, and precious with it. They try to achieve by subterfuge what should be open and straightforward—good and interesting writing *is* what it is, regardless.

There was an Indian restaurant just down the road from the *Stand* offices that we went to regularly—and I went there every day I was in Leeds. They had a good range of vegan and vegetarian options and catered for the omnivores as well. At one lunch meeting with Arc, it was obvious tensions between the Arc crew and Michael went deeper than I had thought—especially for Tony Ward, respected left-winger who started publishing poetry back in the 1960s, a true revolutionary printer/publisher in the vein of the British radical printer/publishers of the 1790s, for whom loyalty is rule number one. Michael had been a good editor for them but had a dream of running his own poetry publishing house. Eventually he would, with the short-lived Leviathan press and journal. I was the new international editor at Arc and had the role of devil's advocate—a go-between and a usurper was not one I enjoyed. Michael's way of handling such situations is to start cracking unsavoury jokes. Which is what he did while he drank his beer.

In our efforts to boost the profile of *Stand*—or maybe to broaden its demographic—we devised a series of ad hoc literary events and participated in a variety of festivals and readings. One—the *Stand* Cambridge University Festival of

American Writing—stands out in my memory because it did not go down well with the *Stand* trustees at all (it wasn't Leeds and didn't honour Jon Silkin, though I am sure he would have enjoyed it).

The Cambridge event was significant in terms of the array of writers we managed to gather. The event was staged at King's College, though participants were billeted in a number of other Cambridge colleges as well. Michael's overwhelming response to the weekend he helped organise was a disappointment with the sizes of the audiences. Full back-page ads in the *London Review of Books* seemed to bring no more than sixty to the main afternoon and between thirty and forty to most sessions. Such are poetry audiences! I was somewhat irritated, thinking Michael a grass-is-always-greener kind of guy.

Americans in Cambridge who are not there for scholarly purposes are similar to but also different from Australians in Cambridge—there's a mixture of an effort to respect the ancient ways and to mock them as trivial and trite (depending on company). Awe and amusement (or bemusement). Australians tend to have louder colonial echoes to deal with, so the sycophancy or the rejection often tend to be more extreme.

The *New Yorker* session and American poet Sharon Olds's reading were two of the stand-outs for me. I had been reading Sharon Olds's work for many years. Her reputation for shocking readers with her clear and concise renderings of private family stories, of the horror of familial witness, of a violent struggle with her religious upbringing, means that most kids interested in contemporary poetry in (American) English will come across her eventually! *Satan Says* is one of those books that etches itself into the domestic with more perversity than it actually contains. It is its own frustrated persona, and an impossible weight to live up to. The process of witness is inverted—we witness 'her' witnessing; and, in the effort to shock, become over-familiarised.

Sharon Olds is an imposing woman, and a sense of marginalised but intense Christian religiosity pervades the atmosphere around her, whether that is her nature or not. Her long hair and longish face seem to fill the space from ceiling to floor. There's an intensity to the illusion. I had corresponded with her about the conference, and her notes were friendly and lively, her writing sharp. But talking with her was an unsettling experience. I had my daughter Katherine with me, only nine years old then. Katherine is striking to look at and has a beacon of red hair that Olds immediately homed in on: 'What remarkable hair.' For the ensuing conversation, Olds did not once look directly at me, but addressed her responses to my questions to an increasingly confused Katherine. 'Confused' is a little strong; Katherine had met many poets, writers and intellectuals by that stage, and took it in her stride, but there was a manic electricity, forced into an only apparently laid-back mode, in Olds, that tapped into Katherine's own manic side. Olds hovered over Katherine. We talked about fundamentalist religion; we talked about being part of it, about 'participating', and then choosing your moment to escape. I am not sure how the conversation began.

Do you go to school here? Olds asks Katherine.

Katherine looks to me to see how she should answer. She can answer as she wishes, of course, but she is uncertain of the portent behind the arching and swamping questions.

Yes, she does, I reply to fill the gap.

You have beautiful red hair. It burns.

Yes, it does, I reply to fill the gap.

And so on ...

Bizarre. Though she'd been talking through Katherine, she'd been talking to me. The child as medium? There was something supernatural, something nineteenth-century séance and occultish about it. The Calvinist wrath was being overturned and replaced by spiritualism. Katherine's red hair seem to inflame her enthusiasm, her invocations, prayers and sermons. That's what it was like. I swapped e-mails with Olds, but things stopped, whether coincidentally or not, after I accorded her new book only lukewarm praise in the *Observer*. It wasn't a bad book, but just too much the same. The guilt—wherever directed—had become mundane, and the damage diluted. You can't afford to dilute damage—its impact must increase with each accumulation. The brilliance of poets such as Sharon Olds, Sylvia Plath, Anne Sexton and Robert Lowell is the way they can return to the same material but allow the level of intensity to shift, and the technique to adapt and grow to broaden the scope, hone the lens. There's something telling about Olds's eyelines—the way she didn't look at me. Talking with Tracy and my friend Brenda recently, I am reminded about women avoiding looking at men in order not to give the wrong idea, or to create the possibility of an intimacy they don't want. I've always been loose with my eyes—I look wherever and at whatever I want. When I was first with Tracy, she remarked on how I observed everything. We were walking through Perth from the railway station, down Pier Street, and I was sherry-sodden and living in the Globe Hotel. I noticed something across the road, out of my peripheral vision, and commented on it. That time in Cambridge, though, Olds wasn't just retaining custody of the gaze—she was staring at Katherine. I could feel the piercing intensity peripherally. She was also staring at me by not looking at me.

It always seems odd to me to make any 'judgement' on a poet's work, especially when they stand up to tyranny and oppression, as Olds has done recently. Her very public rejection of the Bush government is not an easy position to take in an extremely conservative and hostile America. It is not like late-60s protesting when, though against a seemingly impregnable state apparatus, there were enough of you to apparently have some effect. Not so at all now. People cower.

Returning to Michael, who is never far away …

The Kings Lynn festival makes the finances work by billeting authors with local families. The year I attended with Michael, I stayed with a young farming couple on their property on the inlet, with a petrochemical factory literally a hundred feet away. I've started to write about this experience over the years, but it has never gelled. Not sure where to go with it. Appears in fragments and lines. The billeting was clearly at the young wife's instigation, as she seemed to be positioning herself in the community as an artsy type. And she was. Her husband spent the evening I was there watching the football, which was fine. I watched a little as well. He was taciturn in my company, and not sure what a poet might do to his house or wife, I think. I respected both.

I am never comfortable staying at people's places when on the road, for a few reasons: I am a vegan and that's often seen as difficult (though it's not); I tend to keep weird hours, sleeping little; and I just find it plain awkward. This is not to say I haven't enjoyed staying with people—I have—and the more familiar I am with them, the more I tend to feel relaxed. Really, it's about missing my family. I spend so much of my life away from them that, when I am on my own, I like to be near a phone and to talk for hours with Tracy. About a tenth of what we earn has gone on phone bills! The aloneness actually makes you feel closer, insofar as nothing else is able to interfere with the distanced intimacy.

The billeting wife (we have to go generic here for identity and role-play's sake) had 'little to do with her day', though she cooked and kept an immaculate home under the eyes of the petrochemical smog and gloss. There were three or four houses on the farm and she collected the rents every fortnight, keeping the farm accounts in order. There were some disused houses she was planning to do up for holiday farm-stays. It was her project. I, by default, was another. She didn't know who she'd end up with when volunteering to assist with the festival. She could have ended up with Hans Magnus Enzensberger, or Michael or Peter Porter.

King's Lynn is central English coastline. It is a kind of inner port town located at the mouth of The Wash. The farm was on The Wash. The Wash is the mouth of the River Great Ouse, and beyond it lie the fenlands, so low that pumps must be kept running or it will flood. The whole area was reclaimed by drainage engineers over hundreds of years, and, much like Holland and its dykes, it is land not naturally available. When the Ouse floods, it wipes out much of the east of England. I spent relatively little time on that farm, though the husband did drive me out to the edge of The Wash to look. The chemical plant strangely vanished into the background, but its legacy went deep into the silt. The area thrived and thronged with waterbirds. He seemed proud—his father had managed the farm before him. The chemical plant was built on their land—the land seemed to have been taken off them to build it, but the process had given them financial security all the same …

Most of my time was spent wandering the port. I went on a couple of excursions to King's Lynn with Tracy and Katherine roughly around this period, usually on a Saturday, when the bustling market town came to life. We stopped there briefly, though, on our way to one of our pilgrimage places, which is what it has been for people for over a thousand years: Walsingham. Tracy wrote some of her best poems about this once-great town of faith, and I have written quite a few lines about it. For me, Tracy's poem to John Forbes resonates there (he expressed a wish to go there, preferably by bicycle). But back to King's Lynn: there are two docks in the port—Alexandra Dock closest to the river; then, adjoining that and linked by a narrow passage, Bentinck Dock. Along both of these are electric travelling cranes, pieces of machinery that I search out, that have fascinated me around the world. I tried to go to sea when I was seventeen, but couldn't get union permission. The trick of surviving festivals is to find another interest in the immediate locale.

Michael, on the other hand, spent his time socialising, drinking with participants and talking up the journal. Many would laugh to hear me exclude myself from the networking frenzy—I also enjoy talking things over and getting intense, but then I disappear and go to myself, go to the place. I don't want people, any people. Michael stays with people. I remember a brief conversation with British poet Ruth Padel about getting away—I am not sure where she went. Like many of my friends in the past, I think Michael thought of me being something of a piker.

Michael got married in 2005. I know nothing of his wife and knew nothing of the marriage. I guess, since the demise of our editorship at *Stand*, we've moved apart.

10

Shock and awe

FOR PART OF EVERY YEAR we live in Ohio. The locals will smile and greet you, they will help out if there's a family crisis. Many have American flags on their cars and houses, and the houses gleam white even in bad weather. It's the mid-west, heartland of America. Where we live is slightly outside the usual—one of America's iconic private liberal arts colleges set among hills, forest and corn fields. A river meanders by in the valley, and old railway lines have been replaced with asphalted walk trails overarched by trees still bare with winter. The Iraq war is a long way from here physically and mentally, and the locals want to keep it that way.

Don't misunderstand: other than a handful of vocal opponents, there are many who will say 'the war should stop', but they, in the main, go about their business hoping the sun will shine. They are the people you'd want to help you out in a family crisis, even if you were somewhat bemused by their ability to let the world flow on by. There are many, however—and we are rapidly discovering they are the bulk of the people—who will support their government's course of action no matter how much of a problem it might become. The more flawed it seems, the more the heartlanders will, in compensation, go against even their contrary instincts and support it.

This is to do with patriotism. Patriotism is seen as collective responsibility, and, as one bumper sticker says, 'peace is patriotic': so you can be patriotic and opposed to war. This is how a peace march can become a space for patriotism: U.S.A. U.S.A. U.S.A. chanted as a mantra of collective responsibility. The concern is for peace, but this is as an adjunct to patriotic commitment. These are the peace-wanters, in their vocal and silent variations. There are plenty here who see war against everyone who is not of their community as inevitable. It's not only the Muslim other they are wary of, even 'reconciled' to fighting, but the Feds, the feminists, the socialists and the 'tree huggers'. They stockpile weaponry and hone their social skills in deer-hunting season.

It sounds like something taken straight from the *Deliverance* cliché book, but it is there, and you ignore it at your peril. I had the experience of being invited out for some shooting practice, because it was known that as a child in the country I did my fair share of shooting and destroying. I told the incredibly genial guy who offered, that I had given up that stuff well over twenty years ago and I would never touch a gun now—in fact, as a pacifist, I am against all forms of aggression. He was bemused, but continued: 'You'd love it if you tried it again.' He then told me of his friends getting ready for the day of reckoning, whenever that might be, and their preparations for this (food and weapon stockpiling, teaching their kids). '*Bring them on* is what my buddies say,' he added.

A guy who gave me a lift to the city said about the Iraq war: 'When I start to feel it at the gas pump I know something is going on.' And it's true that, like Australia, this is a car-obsessed society—it's considered a basic right to have cheap gas and to be able to buy a car on terms. There is no doubt here that the war is oil-based. There are some who will point out the hypocrisy of the fact that the Americans supplied and supported Saddam's 'weapons of mass destruction' programmes in the late 1970s and early 80s, and that some of those involved in this hold positions of power in the Bush administration. There are others who scoff at the imperialist intentions behind the industrial–military complex's desire to 'democratise' the world, and a few who believe that exploiting the tragedy and suffering of the World Trade Center destruction to further imperialist foreign policy is an insult to the memory of the dead.

What's astonishing, though, in this place where the Constitution (that living, breathing document) and the Bill of Rights are held as the core of identity, is that there's such a lack of awareness that since 9/11, people's rights have been steadily eroded. America is a very different place now.

People are generally afraid to speak out—if they are not indifferent to begin with. In our private college space, the more liberal-minded staff will allow students to articulate their concerns and discomfort, but lessons roll on as usual. Visitors come in, are wined and dined and praised, then return to their distant homes.

We invited an ex-poet laureate here—an internet man of the people. Many whispered that he would be a suitable inspiration at a time like this, without rubbing people's faces in it. I have no idea what he said because, on principle, I could not bring myself to hear such an overt nationalist, however he dressed it up. Maybe he spoke against the war; I have no idea. I hope he did!

In what ways can one speak in a college environment in the heartlands? With my poetry students I have talked about the new sublime (the Hubble telescope with its repaired mirror is the mediator of the new sublime, as is reverence for a polluted ocean or the destruction of the battlefield via the war-making CNN or Fox or MSNBC) and about how a desperate desire for beauty and awe leads people to look to brutality. We read anti-war poems: Native American poems, poems from the Western battlefields of the First World War, and from indigenous Australian poets who have experienced the warfare of 'settlement'.

It is not coincidental that the American battle tactics are called 'Shock and Awe'. This is part of a reconciling of reason and romanticism that marks the twenty-first century. Video games have become its ultimate fetishised manifestation. One of my students said she couldn't write because of media stress, another that she couldn't make sense of the conflicting information, and another that it didn't affect him at all, even though he had a few buddies over there. Most of the others discussed the language of the media and the irony of reporters being 'embedded'—the sexual subtext doesn't seem much of a subtext as they grow excited by the battle.

It seemed to all that the media make war. And the military's usurpation of language, so readily digested by the media, is part of their campaign to conquer their own population as well as the enemy. A 'decapitation strike' decapitates the word or language itself. The murder of language, the reduction of meaning to visual and reactive symbols, is part of the same defamiliarisation, desensitising that 'condones' war in the first place. It is part of the killing process. The naming of weapons using Native American words or associations is part of the process of desensitising: 'Apache' helicopters, 'tomahawk' missiles, and so on, suggest a connection with an authenticating indigenous past, a connection to land that reinforces patriotism ('patriot' missiles), and that effectively whitewashes the theft and murder that accompanied the invasion and occupation of Native American lands.

The reconfiguring of language goes hand in hand with a militarism that translates the word *invasion* into 'Operation Iraqi Freedom', as lucrative post-war 'reconstruction' contracts—which have been in the works since the 1990s—are debated. In a world of repressive regimes, Iraq has the oil to pay for its 'reconstruction': it's worth invading and destroying, without UN approval, by a coalition of profiteers.

There are students having their own say. Provided with a forum, they work it out among themselves. But forums, other than of their own making, are not generally there. And it's worth noting it was in this state that the Kent State massacre took place during the Vietnam War. People here are afraid of protest. 'In the sciences, we can never discuss issues,' one said.

I have been asked many times why Australia so willingly goes where America goes. I tell them about the Second World War, the split with the British over Churchill's unwillingness to allow Australian troops to withdraw from the Middle East for 'home defence'. That split was definitive—as John Curtin said, 'Without any inhibitions of any kind I make it quite clear that Australia looks to America.' The students are astonished to find that Australians fought in Vietnam. 'Are Australians in the Gulf?' I'm afraid so. John Howard was on the television the day before yesterday, assuring all that he would like to be at Camp David with his co-conspirators Bush and Blair but that at such a sensitive time he should be back home, more or less guarding the fort. It was ludicrous. Here, he is considered not a world statesman but one of the mass Other who are on America's side, as opposed to the mass Other who are the enemy. His voice, some say, reminds them of the 'crocodile hunter's'.

On a visit back to Australia, I participated in a massive anti-war march in Perth. Its size was three times the media estimates, and it was genuinely peaceful. I was proud to be part of it. I am told now that the mood has changed, that because 'we're at war', a level of acceptance has crept in. How is war made acceptable by a government acting without consideration of the electorate's original mood? They see themselves as making tough decisions. A tough decision would have been *not* to support this folly.

When our daughter first went to school in Ohio she was asked: 'Do they have radio in Australia?' And my partner was asked in a shop: 'What language do they speak in Australia?—you have very good English.' Yet this was even after the Sydney Olympics! Such moments are irrelevant to the issue in many ways but they do emphasise the inward-looking nature of the regional here in the heartlands.

This community is primarily white and agrarian and is part of the so-called Bible Belt. Churches and meeting halls carry patriotic and sometimes war-mongering signs for passers-by to contemplate. The rare anti-war signs outside various houses were removed (or stolen?) on the first day of conflict.

A mass college e-mail message from a faculty member arrives; it talks of 'defenders of the world's security' and about how we must all think of 'America's sons and daughters'. The other day, a student sent out a link to what he considered a particularly good visual slideshow of bombing and destruction. There are increasingly few mass college e-mail messages protesting the war. To send them would be considered unpatriotic, regardless of one's 'politics'. And as one academic said to me recently, objecting to my desire not to read poems on an awards night as protest against the war: 'Let them [the students] have their moment in the sun.'

It is frightening, truly frightening. I now understand the visual cast of David Lynch's films from the inside out.

11

London

I WAS LOOKING for the River Café in London, on the Thames.

> I wander thro' each charter'd street,
> Near where the charter'd Thames does flow ...

Or the alternative draft of Blake's 'London':

> I wander thro' each dirty street
> Near where the dirty Thames does flow ...

I ended up wandering along the banks of the Thames in W6. Thames Wharf. I couldn't find Rainville Road and felt like I was in a transplanted scene from *Performance* or *Blow-Up*, only gentrified. Flats leant out over concrete paths, their chevroned rooms of glass soaking up all the dirty river-light they could. Maybe a cubist nightmare, with concrete and veneered wood or steel frames making all angles, painted yellow and red and white. I walked down a lane and a couple of guys, hooded, were doing a deal. Didn't seem like the place. A few years before, I'd ended up in a Yardie crack house in East London, stolen BMWs and Uzi sub-machine guns, and it could have been there, but this area stank of wealth. And art.

When I found the café, I found Blixa Bargeld and a woman I imagined was his girlfriend seated there. A round table in front of the bar, vast feature window, a whole wall of glass. Shaded against the light, if I recall. Blixa had a hat tilted *Clockwork Orange*-style over one eye. And a lock of German Expressionist hair. Maybe from one of my favourite early German films. Some have called him one of the greatest guitarists of the last two decades: an off-key melody that's his own cutting through Nick Cave's psycho-sublimities with the Bad Seeds. I admire his work there, but it's with the German group Einstuerzende Neubauten that he's really affected me. I first saw them on TV in the late 80s, playing jackhammers and other heavy equipment in a Japanese warehouse. Industrial music. Brilliant. And the lilting lyrics of later work, 'You will find me if you want me in the garden ...' And it was theatre, and it was anarchic, even nihilist at times. The *Hamletmaschine* was a revelation.

The scene I'd walked through getting to the River Café would form one of the backdrops of *The Wasps*, a later play of mine written in and about Cambridge. The conversation

I had with Blixa and his companion was a touchstone. I knew I *had* to work with him. For almost a decade we've been trying to make it happen. I see him in China soon, and we have the project: America. We're almost rolling. But we began with Gilgamesh, his idea. I wrote a few starter-texts, maybe he did some music. Then I wrote 'Seed Ethics' for him, maybe some music. I am not sure where the beginnings are. George Steiner, the eminent academic and critic, says in the beginning of his *Grammars of Creation*: 'We have no more beginnings.' Blixa's work, rather than about collapse and open-endedness, always struck me as being about holes. I think that's also what I work with as a poet. His conceptual and aesthetic landscapes are entered and exited by holes, as are my physical landscapes.

Blixa seemed relaxed as he took off his hat and rested it on the corner of a table. I started to wonder whether the woman was Blixa's girlfriend or his assistant, as she looked after the paraphernalia. She started taking notes, then started drawing wildly on the tablecloth. She said nothing, or very little. It was eerie. She was intense, and it seemed to amuse Blixa that she disturbed me. Moving between languages, he was a quick thinker. And complex. Manic, as always, I plied him with ideas. They were considered, and filtered, and to be kept for consideration later. Blixa is not just artistic energy and style, he's also theatre management. He knows his business. He's an actor and writer, a composer and musician.

It was a long lunch. The drawing on the tablecloth continued. Caricatures, text. Speech balloons. We discussed a young Czech novelist, (the woman's ex?), who'd recently committed suicide. The woman drew looks from around the restaurant. With her dark hair and fallen-angel face, each smile broke a line of thought. Appetisers, main meal, desserts. Drinks. I took the check. To my shock, it was the equivalent of over 500 Australian dollars. I looked at Blixa and the woman. It's a good restaurant, she said. Speaking. Not sure how to react, she slid the tablecloth carefully from beneath the dishes and folded it in quarters. There, that's for you to keep. Payment for their 'share' of the bill, I guess. I kept the docket.

Recently, I asked Blixa who the woman was. Amanda Ooms. Swedish actress. I recall that for a while she went out with a Swedish punk rock star who posed when he was a teenager for a hardcore porn magazine, and that fans used to throw the issues of the mag onto the stage while he performed. I looked Ooms up on the internet and found many nude celebrity shots featuring her in a variety of positions excised from her films. She's not a porn star but being a great 'beauty' the net has turned her into one.

I e-mailed her to ask of her memories of the occasion, and she got back to me with an interesting reply:

Yes … Is her virtue.
    A memory is holy and impeccable. If you want to. So, river café. Two gentlemen and a lady. Two gentlemen filled with the endless blaze bouncing against the endless hunt for some kind fulfilment. When it in the end come down to the conversation,

observation and touch. The conversation was fierce
and well spoken, as I remember circling. It is true
that through language the other changes, he says
something different and another world opens which
is the others. The observation is how it all settles
and brings time forwards. And then the touch, this
is why the lady is there. Either you touch her, or
you want to. And then there was this journey in to
the sacred garden of beautiful wine and the food
that you can get at good restaurants but honestly
it's all happening in the kitchen. Blixa knows how
to make the black pasta with the ink. He knows
how to make it happen. The lady knows how to
make trembling food that makes your cheeks glow.
The poet knows how to listen and to remember
how to remember. It was all good.
A. Ooms

12

Jacques Derrida

I HAVE LOST a lot of my books over the years—in my drug and alcohol days they were sold in their thousands to feed habits; in my travelling days they were given away or simply lost. From the mid-1990s I have managed to hold on to most books, even if dispersed across three continents, and, along with clothes and a computer, they are pretty well all that I own. I don't want to own more, and even the half-share I have in a car is a burden to me. One book I have held onto, and which has travelled around the world with me, is a gift from the French philosopher Jacques Derrida in 1996. *What is Poetry?* A German edition set in French, German, Italian and English, it became a beginning for us both; and, after his death, a persistence. I like to keep my side of things going.

I can't recall why I originally wrote to Jacques. But I did, and he responded.

Yes, I recall, it was about *What is Poetry?* We agreed that I would write poems, which he would discuss in razor-like commentaries. A Rime of the Ancient Mariner.

It had been many years since I was previously in Paris—probably twelve or so years. For Tracy and me it was our first trip outside England after moving there, and Jacques was a big reason for going. We met by the Ecole des Hautes Etudes en Sciences Sociales, where he worked, and walked to a café close by.

We talked about the possibility of translating his works. I asked what he thought of the translation by Gayatri Chakravorty Spivak of *Of Grammatology*. He said: You mean Spivak's *Of Grammatology*—joke being that it was more her work than his. He did not say it with vehemence, but with that impish smile so often observed about him. 'Impish' comes across as diminutive, and indeed he was small, with a Peter Falk face, but so charismatic he loomed large. He deprecated his own ability to read and speak English—it was entirely functional, good even.

Jacques was a radical in ways that people are unwilling or unable to recognise—not only of the ilk of Czechoslovakia in the 1980s and other actions of protest as well as his protest against constructs in language through deconstruction, but in his poetics. Above all else he loved poetry. He believed poetry was hope, and he was deeply proud that his son was a poet and medieval scholar. I am not sure if it was on that visit, or a later one, that he spoke excitedly of how his son and others had published an annual poetry volume that sold in vast numbers, was discussed on television and had entered the daily cultural conversations of Paris. What was unusual about this excitement was that when it came to discussing his own attentions from the outside world, he was politely ironic and diminishing of his role. Never of his ideas—he was rock-solid behind them; they were his honesty—but gently mocking of his public persona. Like so many French intellectuals, though ashamed of the travesties of American democracy, he enjoyed his time out of the decay of old Europe and his teaching periods in America. California seemed to glow in his conversation.

I asked him if he would visit Cambridge, maybe speak if I set up an event for him. He muttered quietly that he was not liked in Cambridge, and seemed hurt when he related that they'd turned him down for an honorary degree. What made it worse was that those who'd called him a philosophical fraud were centred in my College, Churchill. I said I would challenge them. This never really happened because no one at Churchill, or anywhere else, seemed willing to discuss it. Jacques started talking to Katherine, who sat drinking a juice and swinging her legs on the plush red velvet seat. She said something about Spain and the storks, still big in her mind. Within months she had adopted a Cambridge accent. This he found faintly amusing. He was pleasant and patient with her. Tracy talked about translating. He said to her: You have the best French spoken by a non-native I have ever heard.

I later took the conversation back to his son. I know Pierre a little, I said. He's a unique poet. And indeed he is—

a book published not long after that meeting in English translation was entitled *Personal Pong*. I managed to get a batch of poems from him for *Salt* magazine which I published in English.

How do you know Pierre? asks Jacques.

I met him at last year's Cambridge Conference of Contemporary Poetry. I wasn't sober then. I am now.

Oh? What happened? he smiled, an eye dropping in that Columbo way.

There was a party at the notoriously difficult Stephen Rodefer's place. A tiny one-bedroom flat not far from the university. I think he bought it with money he got for a residency at one of the Cambridge colleges. Maybe it was Gonville and Caius. I spent most of the conference talking with his photographer wife because she seemed the most together. She told me not to trust poets.

Poets are honest!

Yes, in their writing.

True.

(I am reconstructing this to suit the flow, but that was the gist of it.)

I continued:

At the party, Pierre talked about recent French poetry and politics. Someone whispered to me that he was the son of Jacques Derrida but that he didn't want anyone to know.

Jacques looked proud but a little hurt: He makes his own way. He doesn't need me.

The party itself degenerated and the only person who behaved more diabolically than myself was Rodefer. I have a soft spot for Rodefer, as many do, but I think he is dangerous. Brilliant poet, as the wandering American with enough money to live on and never have to work, who segued into a European avant-garde and drinks at least as much as he writes, he is constantly insulting people as they read, and creating fights. At one conference he yelled out to me, 'You fucked my wife.' I hadn't. I did walk a lot with her, though. And then he said it again and again and insisted. I cross his path every now and again—at Strawberry Fair in Cambridge, where he listens to punk bands, or hanging around young female students with an avant-garde drink-camaraderie, talking about how little he is published. He reminds me of John Forbes. Watching them meet was weird—a mirror job. They kind of liked each other, though there was clearly a macho rivalry. (Rodefer spoke French, though, and John wanted to speak French, and to say fuck off to the French.)

We met Jacques Derrida again at a reading I gave at the Maison de la Poésie in Paris, with Tracy reading an introduction in French to my work, and actors reading translations of my poems. We spent the afternoon looking through the Pompidou—I remember Alexander Calder sculptures more than anything else. And Yves Klein blue. The tubes and gantries of the Pompidou made me think of old church crypts, not technology. Still, I keep going back there, getting my fix. We walked around the area looking for the Maison, to speak to the people before the reading. We went back over to the Left Bank—walking past Notre Dame, place of my Easter escape in 1984, running from the Finnish secret police who had told me to leave Helsinki and Finland, full of opium, whiskey and Bertolt Brecht—to an Egyptian restaurant that did couscous and grilled vegetables. We went there often over the years. We were staying in a small apartment. There were problems with our hosts. I bought a lot of baguettes. I wrote most of the stories of *Grappling Eros* in that apartment. In the Panthéon we watched Foucault's Pendulum; the crypts sent Katherine crazy. No, this time we were in a hotel. We caught the métro into the city, to the Maison. Quite a few stops out. On the outer circles. The next day Katherine was sick—no more babysitting—and we spent the next couple of evenings sitting in the hotel room, watching George Steiner on television.

When Katherine was finally better we took the train to Fontainebleau. There are photos of us walking down the avenues there. I planned a book in which stories on each stop of the metro would segue into poetry. I have written that work about railway stations in Perth now, not in Paris, but that's where the idea and inspiration came from. We went to the Maison and there was a good turnout and the organisers were very excited because Derrida was in the audience. He sat on his own, with no one daring to sit next to him. It was odd to see. After the event a number of us went to a nearby café and Jacques waited until others had been seated before slipping in beside Tracy and me. I can talk to the others any time, he said, but not to you. I want to talk about the echidnas. That may seem weird, but Derrida and I were seriously fascinated by them. He said he'd been working on his side of things. I have never seen this work—these annotations written to accompany my poems (I wrote many for him over the years); I wonder if it's in his archive. He stayed for about two hours and then said he must go home to his wife, as she was expecting him and he didn't spend enough time at home as it was. He complimented us about the reading and took his leave. Nothing dramatic.

Six months later I was in Paris for a night, on the way through to Toulouse. I rang Jacques the morning my train was to leave, and told him I had had a dream that he was John Donne, that he had written his philosophy as poems by John Donne. He grew animated in a way I'd never heard him, to the point where his voice broke up as he shifted rapidly between a stilted English and quickfire French. In essence, he had been working to bring out a French translation of Donne with a poet who must have recently died, and for whom Jacques had had much admiration. He wanted to see his Donne appear. He talked about Donne's poetry—about its wit, science and creativity. The metaphysics seemed metaphor for the spirit behind his own views of language and culture. Later, I wrote him a dream-letter as I often dreamt about him, and sometimes dream dreams consisting of nothing but the words of *The Gift of Death* or some other Derrida work.

'DECONSTRUCTING JACQUES DERRIDA: THE MOST REVILED PROFESSOR IN THE WORLD DEFENDS HIS DIABOLICALLY DIFFICULT THEORY'—Mitchell Stephens, *Los Angeles Times Magazine*, July 21, 1991, Sunday:

> The world's most controversial living philosopher, arguably its most controversial living thinker, is sitting at a concrete picnic table at an outdoor snack bar at UC Irvine. Few of the undergraduates who stroll by in jams or jeans seem to notice Jacques Derrida, with his carefully tailored grey suit and purple tie. Few would recognize his name if they were introduced.
>
> But as Derrida sips his coffee from a plastic cup, a crowd of world-class graduate students and star professors from as far away as China is already hustling for the best seats in his classroom. In a few minutes, Derrida will present two immensely difficult hours on the latest applications of his renowned method—deconstruction—and that room full of scholars will barely allow itself a cough.
>
> Echoes of Derrida's ideas can now be heard in the most unlikely places. The word deconstruction (albeit shorn of much of its meaning) now appears in newspaper reviews and at dinner parties: 'Let's deconstruct this scene.' It is becoming, like existentialism before it, a part of the language—to the point where a State Department official can speak of a plan for the 'deconstruction' of part of the

American Embassy in Moscow, and Mick Jagger can ask, 'Does anyone really know what deconstructivist means?' ('Deconstructivist' has been the most controversial variety of architecture in recent years.) But the main impact of Derrida's method has been felt on college campuses.

Deconstruction—which Derrida gave birth to in Paris in the 1960s—swept through American universities in the '70s and '80s, presuming to remake nothing less than the way professors and students perform their most basic activity: reading.

This is an example of the kind of journalism masquerading as knowledgeable irony that has infuriated me over the years. It (intentionally) diminishes Jacques Derrida's thinking and achievement by creating a cult of celebrity, treating the philosopher as a purveyor of product not unlike the way paparazzi portray movie stars caught topless on the Riviera. Derrida is sold in so many ways as the 'Father of Deconstruction', as if deconstruction were pure method, which, for Derrida, it never was.

Then there is the subtle 'racial' othering of Derrida, complete with a quote from another prominent Jewish intellectual (a critic who is also often misused textually), Harold Bloom, in Stephens' article:

Derrida's dark mediterranean skin contrasts with a wide, still full frame of silver hair. 'Striking,' one of his female graduate students had commented, twice.

The word most of his friends use to describe him is 'gracious.' 'Jacques is the mildest of persons,' adds Yale professor Harold Bloom. Nevertheless, Derrida is occasionally unwilling or unable to play the roles expected of him. I had been warned that he would not respond well in particular to personal questions of the sort the subject of a magazine profile must face. 'Ah, you want me to tell you things like "I-was-born-in-a-petit-bourgeois-Jewish-family-which-was-assimilated-but …"' is how Derrida parried one such query by a French magazine reporter. 'Is this really necessary? I just can't do it,' he protested to that reporter.

Jacques Derrida's refusal to play is played against him. Does that matter in the face of it? Probably not. But what's put to the public test is the idea of a writer whose life is the idea. People often had an opinion about him without having ever read him. What's on trial here is the cult of celebrity which devalues ideas.

Jacques Derrida's Jewish heritage was pivotal to his experience and the way he saw the world (he was expelled from his original school in Algeria because of this). I think that his interest in Tracy and myself was to do with our difference in Europe—as Australians, we only partly fitted, and as Australians of European heritage, we logically looked back to where we didn't really fit. Any texts I gave him to 'annotate' were deconstructions to begin with. He would laugh when I used the term because he didn't want our interactions to be critiques of his work. I have always been astonished by the extent to which reporters simply didn't *get* him. I suppose they were lulled by his willingness to talk, his generosity that would leave room for him to be misunderstood. In working against binary interpretations, Derrida opened a space for the figurative in science, an epistemology of ambiguity and alternatives in the real. These are not his words, or paraphrases of them, but my way of understanding an interaction, brief but important to me, with a great thinker. For me, he sparked poems, and generated a dialogue within text that couldn't be pinned down.

Kevin Hart, who has written so well on Derrida, and whose writings Derrida appreciated, arranged to get Jacques down to Australia. A couple of people at UWA asked if I could persuade the organisers to allow Derrida to make it to Perth—it didn't work out, as Jacques said he didn't want to travel further. As it was, they had to bring him down first class as he feared the effect of the flight. The same fear has kept Harold Bloom and many other older creative people away from Australia. I heard from Jacques that he enjoyed his visit to Australia, but little else. However, whether or not the anecdote is true, I did hear from a couple of other sources that the very first thing he did upon being met at the airport was to ask to be taken to a zoo to see an echidna!

Although I never knew Jacques well, the friendship, as it was, seemed to matter. He certainly read the books I sent and asked to see ones he knew he hadn't received. I read and discussed and taught his work. Towards his last years we had little contact—maybe I sent him the odd echidna poem. It was a month or so before I heard that, sadly, he had died.

13

Letters to Frieda

I HAD NEVER MET Frieda Hughes, the daughter of Ted Hughes and Sylvia Plath, but when I first read her poetry I thought it very interesting, if 'uneven'. I think it was in spite of her parents that I felt such enthusiasm for her poems. From the moment of publication, Frieda ran the gauntlet of comparison, especially with her mother. It was said that she was but an imitation, a mish-mash of both voices. Even her subject matter was found to be similar. I think it's this judgement that made me really baulk.

Frieda Hughes had spent many years in Wooroloo (the source of her first book's title), maybe an hour or so's drive from York, and Perth. The landscapes I read in the poems were ones I was familiar with, and were often about European incursion into that 'nature', especially in her fox poem (so often compared to her father's great poem about writing). The shock of fire, so common in the 'ranges' area of southern Western Australia near Perth, and the destruction of her studio, were the real impetus to poetry. There are analogies to be drawn with the loss of her mother, but it's that loss by fire and its reclamation through language that drive the work. Auto/biography is to be expected, but this work had taken a long time to appear (Frieda was around forty), because, I imagine, it had to filter these influences on her writing.

For me, the poetry had intensity in itself, but also an intensity that fitted the stories I'd heard of Frieda around Perth, her marriage to the Hungarian Australian, Laszlo Lukacs, an artist of similar intensity, and someone I'd also never met (though Tracy had). Frieda was known in Perth as an artist (as she still is), and the only work of hers I'd come across were cartoons (of cats?) in the weekend *West Australian* newspaper glossy lift-out. They never did much for me. I knew at least one person, a writer of stories, a Plath-obsessive who kept a large poster of Plath in her work space, she told me, who knew Frieda reasonably well. But that was it, until the poems arrived from Neil Astley, editor of the prestigious Bloodaxe Books. I actually read the work then without really being aware of the parentage, which didn't strike me as entirely relevant. And I still maintain this, and maybe I do so alone. I think that's the connection I formed with Frieda from a distance, sketchy as it is. The work seemed so much about loss, about not being able to retrieve what was lost. As one who had left Australia for Britain, I understood the dislocations (in reverse) of her imagery.

I've now met Frieda twice—both times at the 2003 Perth Festival. Once was during a session we did together on myth in our writing. She knew I knew her work well since I'd written about it and 'blurbed' it—but I was pleased (as one is), when she chose an early poem of mine, 'Prometheus', to talk about. Apart from her books *Wooroloo* and *Stonepicker*, she also read from a new manuscript of mythology poems, some of her most powerful work, and had some things in common with my own poetic interests. It was one of the best festival sessions I have done—that is, among the most enjoyable for me. That evening, with Laszlo and a friend of theirs, we sat at a Northbridge café on the street, talking over pretty well every awkward issue there is to talk over. Sex, drugs, and rock and roll, and the horrors of being bullied. I won't repeat the core of what was discussed, but suffice it to say we developed a kind of mutual fascination, I think.

As a result of this interaction, we agreed to start a book of letter–poems, epistles about who we are, what we write, what we are doing. Frieda wrote almost immediately, and I took longer than a year to reply, then another year to send it (by then rewritten). I am not sure why it was so difficult for me, but I think it comes out of really not knowing someone at all on a personal or intimate friendship level, but feeling you know them deeply through their writing. Always a dangerous thing.

I remember telling Frieda about a couple of horrific incidents that took place near where we were sitting in Northbridge. I was sitting close to her, and felt the need to pull my chair back as I told her. She registered this, as she seems to register all body language as it's displayed towards her—a woman who takes notice on the micro level but who gives off a nonchalant air when comfortable, her thick blondish-brown hair controlled, and her eyes the repositories of whatever you might want. I feel guilty even making these observations. Loose tucked-in blouse, jeans. I think she was wearing gold jewellery—large rings as well—but am not sure. Why does it matter? Why should one notice, even remember—I tend to recall these things only vaguely. But I recall things quite precisely with Frieda—the more so, the more I put my mind to it. Many would write that she looked like her mum (and her dad) at that moment, but it didn't cross my mind. Anyway, I told her things I wouldn't tell anyone, and don't know why I did; disarmed. So, here now at the confessional (and I was brought up High Anglican), I will repeat what I told her. That in that Lebanese place I overdosed in the toilets and was taken to Royal Perth Hospital where the doctors told me if I didn't stop I would die. I wasn't joking. She seemed to want to soothe me, but quickly understood that I am one who doesn't like or want soothing. I want to feel intact. And then to leave.

A lot of Frieda's charisma is in her voice (deepish, measured … publicly and socially aware … a kind of poise) and her eyes. At her best, her poems mesmerise and distress, as she does in person. I have no idea if she's ever been told anything like this before. I might be way off the mark, but I think that's why Greek mythology has so fascinated her: a confrontation with the archetypes people and circumstances have imposed on her. She was sceptical of the film about to appear on the subject of her mother and father, as I was about Gwyneth Paltrow playing Sylvia Plath! She talked of her brother and her stepmother, briefly. She talked of how inseparable art and poetry were for her. What left the biggest impression on me, though, was the dynamic between her and Laszlo: he seemed sophisticated (in the European-artist-as-Australian sense; lover of 'good things', a distin-guisher between good and bad, high and low), yet gauche, saying things without thinking—occasionally offensive (which Frieda, sharp as a tack, would tactfully rectify with a 'but, Laszlo …'), waiting for reactions to the seeds he'd sown: he seemed to spark her up, to watch over her, but also needed her to fix up his faux pas. He seemed the carer, at least in that public dynamic, but not quite sure how really to play such a role.

> 1st December 2003.
> Dear John,
> Counting Blessings.
> I put aside the idea of
> A letter-poem in May, in answer
> To your email—to visit
> A friend in Melbourne
> Who was dying of cancer.
> We'd visit Laszlo's father too,
> But a week before we left we knew
> He was dead, his wife
> Too boiled in spite to grieve,

Having kept him broken-legged
In the bed, a fortnight until
A blood-clot got him
And he could finally leave.
We visited death every day
As it took up residence in our friend's face,
Her skin, its mask,
The scar on her bald skull
Not as wide as her smile,
Her fingers knitting up her past,
Her present and the time left last
As she spoke, as frank as the saw
That cut her head open,
As if she'd knit up the cranial hole
And restrain her evaporating soul.
Hours with her were delicate straws – like glass,
Clasp too hard and all that's left
Are scars and shards to mark the loss.
Back in England whole dead trees
Piled on the mat by the mailbox,
Sliced, pulped and rollered through printers,
They'd collected in heaps. It took weeks
To undo all the things delayed
Until I got back to letters in May.
We forgot our wedding anniversary
For the seventh time today.
I was reminded by dating
The back of a dog painting,
Realising she was as old as our marriage.

We ate pizza from cardboard
And drank Veuve Clicquot
From fish-stemmed glasses,
Bought on a walk in New York,
And for a few moments watched
Each other's colours sink
Back into the stain
Of our outlines, illuminating
Our deep breath before the next
Upheaval scatters our purpose again.
Love
Frieda.

October, 2005.
Hi, F.
Belatedly—very belatedly,
I am replying to your letter-poem,
your epistle. I am working on a book
with the working title *First Meetings
with Poets*, and you're the subject
of one of the chapters. And that
got me to thinking about text
as the first and truest
of meetings, that 'in-person'
supplements the poems,
the emails … increasingly,
and not the other way around.
But then, whole friendships
have been historically

conducted through letters—
Elizabeth Barrett, though she finally
met her close but distant neighbour,
Boyd, becoming his scribe …
At the moment, for me, it's all neologisms.
Oh, I did draft an earlier letter—god,
it would be over two years ago now,
not long after receiving yours …
ironically, I'd just got back
from outside Australia—there's Australia,
and then there's 'outside Australia'—
as you know—when a horrendous accident
(choppers, numerous police cars,
even a crane to remove steel rods that had broken loose
from a semi—we later heard it was the local
MP's wife who had been crushed
under the *vernichteten* weight) caused
all traffic to be diverted before the Chidlows turn-off,
via Wooroloo, onto the Great Eastern Highway,
then back south to the Lakes to hook up
with the Great Southern Highway …
I drove down the Great Southern this morning …
three days on the same road I suffered a kind of death,
sucked into vacuum by a speeding truck,
blanking out and thinking hell,
I'm caught in some kind of vortex,
I'm still driving, but driving dead …
seriously, no joke …
full moon has meant roos out

and the gravel shoulders
are littered with carcasses
caught in that supine praying position
(there's no parody in this) ...
I can't stop thinking about Paul Celan's 'ichten',
and the paranoia that keeps you constantly
looking in the mirror, watching out
for police traps ...
looped together in myth,
we can't talk our way out of allegory
or cause and effect,
as trapped in the body of text
is the archetypal flower
that pokes its head up
to be lopped off: I saw this
when the birds undid the sheep,
when the sheep ate the grass
and there was nothing left.
Love, JK

14

Faith no more?

IN 1991, *Meanjin* literary journal from Melbourne ran a special issue on Language poetry—one of the most influential single issues of a literary journal ever run in Australia, I'd guess. I had come across Language poetry before, but it was certainly this issue that confirmed my interest in the work of Lyn Hejinian, Charles Bernstein, Bruce Andrews and Carla Harryman. I'd also had my interest caught by having a few poems published in unseen small-scale photocopied journals coming out of New York and San Francisco. The really significant event, ironic in the anti-cult of personality ascribed to Language, was the visit (visitation) to Perth of the ur-Language poet Lyn Hejinian in 1995. Not long after that, I published a volume of her poetry—*Guide, Grammar, Watch and the Thirty Nights*—with Folio (Salt)

Publishing in Australia. It went hand in hand with an article I'd published on Language poetry, which elicited one of the most twisted and egomaniacal responses I've ever received, in a letter from a Melbourne poet demanding I rewrite it to mention his work. The passion and politics of language.

I've always been a fan of Faith No More, and when Lyn Hejinian mentioned her friend 'Mike Patton' during question time after her reading at Curtin University, I knew we had a lot to talk about. Her work fascinated me because it seemed to move beyond the mere denial of self with a repositioning of the self in the poem. From a founding Language poet, it says something about the constant misclassifications of the 'movement' in the first place. I can't recall how I ended up going across to her motel, but maybe I drove her back from the reading and I asked her to sign some books, or maybe she offered to lend me some. I've remembered that interaction because of her polite nervousness when I entered her private space. She is a delicately-built woman with intense eyes, and one can tell that her personability has come through fixing people with a look and holding it. Her eyes tend towards the large, and close when angry, though it's their limpidity that invites you to talk. Her dress is (or was) caftan-like, shifts that cover and yet give an air of femininity. A gendered de-gendering. Her hair was ample and protected her from intrusion. Friendly but also keeping me at a distance, she showed me a manuscript she was working on. It hit me: each letter was placed neatly in a tiny square of the graph paper it was written on, with texts crossing over and going off at right angles. The page was measured but alive, the contradiction between the mathematical and organic that's at the core of her work. I liked her. I got the sense that she was used to having the attentions of younger male acolytes, that she enjoyed the mothering mentoring role. I told her about the family farm and, like many writers, she expressed a desire to see some 'outback Australia'.

I picked Lyn up from her hotel. I seem to recall that it was a crystal blue morning, not particularly warm. As we drove out of the city, she told me about her jazz saxophonist husband Larry, about her adopted children, and about the foundation she and her husband had set up. I liked the mix of poet and conscience, not so common in my experience. She talked about San Francisco and I said I'd visit her if the American government would ever let me in—mentioning how I'd been refused because of my drug and activism record, how I'd told the CIA interviewer via phone from Bangkok that I never inhaled … I told her a little about that side of my life, and she replied with stories of people she'd known with similar troubles.

For some reason I had two cowboy western comics I'd managed to salvage from that period, or maybe I told her about them. I didn't read comics, though I had done so avidly as a child. In fact, I'd had a major comic collection. These I'd picked up for twenty cents at a second-hand bookshop because I wanted to write some poems based on the idea of the western in Australia—applying an American template to show absurdity and difference, a theme that has been ridden into the ground in film now. Lyn said she'd always been interested in doing something with comics and I promised to post one or two to her. I think I did at some later date. As noted on the *My Life* blog (book's afterlife): 'If I couldn't be a cowboy, then I wanted to be a sailor.'

I can't recall a lot of Lyn's visit to the farm. I did write two long poems in response to it, though. One refers to the cemetery, so I guess we spent time there. In fact, I think it's an addiction we shared. Was it before or after she told me about going to an autopsy with Mike Patton? Something I found weird and distasteful, but she found relevant.

The next time I saw Lyn was in San Francisco at a reading organised by Kevin Killian and Dodie Bellamy as part of Small Press Traffic. Kevin and Dodie, like decadents from a Huysmanic Paris, were people towards whom artists gravitated . I had not long been 'straight' and they represented the closest crossover I'd encountered between the old world of substance addiction and extreme behaviour, and the staidness of Cambridge where I'd been living. This visit to the United States was made shortly after returning to Cambridge for our permanent move there—Tracy and Katherine were still at Jeremy and Suze Prynne's while I was touring on my Young Australian Creative Fellowship (which came complete with publicist in New York: the regal Selma Shapiro). San Francisco was an awakening, and I'd go back twelve months later to do a reading at the Modern Language Association for the Australian Studies people.

During my time at Cambridge I'd been working on a book via the fax machine with sculptor and novelist Urs Jaeggi, whom I'd met a year earlier, at a PEN conference in Fremantle, Western Australia, and would later stay with in Berlin. Urs was a Swiss living in Berlin (he now lives in Mexico), who had turned his back on conventional art and writing, despite a massive success and fame, and now wrote avant-garde pieces nobody wanted to publish. Prior to that, he'd been a professor at Berlin Free University, where in the 1960s he'd been one of the sociologists who developed the theory of ergonomics in the work place.

Urs and I have a mutual fascination for the work of the French philosophers Gilles Deleuze and Félix Guattari, and we chatted about utilising/using their texts, with a variety of languages and texts of our own. We ended up with a collaborative book entirely written via the fax machine. We did this over a period of six months, starting in Berlin and Perth, then Berlin and the Blue Mountains, and finally Berlin and Cambridge (following my movements from fax location to fax location). We finished it, copied it, and sent it to possible publishers, who then lost the work. To this day, the book remains unpublished, and probably lost—though sections were published in Kevin and Dodie's photocopied cult Language poetry journal *Mirage*.

I remember visiting Kevin and Dodie's house in San Francisco where I felt I was in the blooper cut-out scene of a television episode. Both Kevin and Dodie emanate multitudinous contradictory sexual waves—bi and poly and perverse thrown in. I like that. Kevin, walking me up the hill to their place (I think we had bussed there), told me how he was blown away by seeing a small poem of mine, 'The Orchardist', on San Francisco's buses. It had got there by way of a series that John Tranter did for US public transport funded by the Australia Council. Though it pleased me to have the poem seen, read and commented about, what truly surprised me was how enthusiastic this supposed avant-gardist was about what is in reality a simple imagistic poem. So, the division and boundaries and rivalries one had heard so much about were a little less resolute and determined than they were declared to be. It's like the lyric in Lyn Hejinian's 'anti-lyrical' poetry. There are no borders but those we cross, and often we are simultaneously on one side and the other.

I think of Kevin and Dodie as being symbiotically connected, even when Kevin told me he photocopied *Mirage* at work (I couldn't imagine him working in any sort of office, even less, separated from Dodie for any time at all). The inside of their place is not clear in my mind other than the stereo playing, sex books, a small kitchen (small place generally), tassels of some sort, and other people 'chilling'. The 'chilling' aspect might be substituted with other chillings— I don't doubt they were out of it, but I was straight, so not interested. Rather than comparisons with the drug scene of my experience, it reminded me more of the DJ I knew when I was a teenager who introduced me to Crass and the Dead Kennedy's, and whose lounge-room ceiling was 'supported' by yoghurt carton pillars. Or maybe, more recently, a student house (privately rented in the village) at Kenyon

College. But then these weren't students, though maybe old habits die hard. American collegiate life is a rite of passage, and its ways of community extend far into people's lives. I don't know if Kevin and Dodie went to college.

Reading with Lyn that night was a big thrill, as was hearing the other 'Language'-orientated poets in the line-up. I read some 'experimental' stuff but mainly concentrated on my anti-pastorals. Experimentation was tangential for me. I wanted to be with the parrots. The introductions reflected this.

The following day Lyn picked me up with an artist friend of hers and a young acolyte male with whom she was starting a new journal, a replacement for the highly success-ful poetics journal she'd edited with Barrett Waten. No, memory lapse, I actually walked down to a café and met Lyn and her friends there, and then got a lift with them to the New School where Lyn was teaching, and I sat in on a seminar and participated from an Australian perspective. Lyn was examining nineteenth-century American frontier narratives—*Last of the Mohican*s, and so on—and it was fascinating discussing the similarities and differences with Australian efforts in this regard. New School seemed a world away from Cambridge, but its relaxed Haight-Ashbury feel a model to base things on, and the hybridising between the critical and creative 'where it was at'. Heading down to the bohemian-style café with its drapings and incense, I walked through the middle of a robbery, with a guy toting a pistol running past me backwards and keeping the barrel fixed on the opening of a record store he'd just done over. I didn't blink and kept walking. I don't know if I smiled at him, but if I did it was merely a nervous twitch.

I am not really interested in biography, but in the residual nature of friendship and even indifference. Lyn and I are no longer in contact, though I dedicated my recent volume of collected experimental poems to her.

So, I was in San Francisco a year later. That was on New Year's Eve 1997: I remember because the details were sorted out by my then literary agent Bettina Keil, and I listened to the frictions of New Year's from my hotel, taking the odd wander through the surging streets. I heard Adrienne Rich read at that conference, a reading so full that people stood way down the outer corridor to catch a word. Over those days I did a lot of walking, as I am wont to do, and a lot of San Francisco for me comes from then. It was cold. There were many beggars. I bought books down in the city and learnt about the renaissance. I met Marjorie Perloff, first hearing her speak at a session in which she was arguing against the Norton Anthology. From the audience, I think. I went to dinner and met Charles Bernstein, Peter Gizzi, Fanny Howe and others. Lyn introduced me … though I can't really recollect. How much did I have to do with Lyn by then? She was at the dinner, and maybe I met the photographer–artist friend then? Or as well. She might be able to clarify, but I don't want to ask her. Peter Gizzi was introduced to me and I to him as people who had overcome similar past problems. We took one look at each other and knew. He seemed to be on hyper-drive and so did I. That's being straight. Charles

Bernstein told us about his doing an advertisement for the Yellow Pages. A lot of the dinner was about poetry and the mass media. It was a dinner and a half.

Gotham Cities

My American publicist told me, before I went on to read at Segue in Manhattan, that to fail in New York was to be expected, to succeed a rarity. A New York crowd is a hard crowd. It went okay!

At the invitation of Charles Bernstein, one of the central figures of Language poetry in America, I took a plane from New York to Buffalo. Buffalo is really the home of the skyscraper, and the 1930s architecture squats over the city like an anachronistic modernism, a glimpse back through the wormhole into what we might have become. We—all of us—saw Buffalo as the centre of the new imperialism. SUNY—the State University of New York at Buffalo—Charles had told me, was designed so that the students could be funnelled into one concrete area should they riot. The dorms at Kenyon College (don't forget, Kent State is actually in Ohio) were designed with the same riot control issues in mind. I took notes while with Susan Schultz, looking at the city's old grain silos: an inversion of capitalism, the detritus, a wasteland as oppressive as the collapsed junkyard economies of the old Soviet Bloc. Here are a few of those notes (they eventually became a poem), direct from the diary:

8/11/1996

Buffalo

Gotham city decay elevated up & downtown with
ethnic allocation, art deco stations of a neglected
cross that could become the Polish Community
Centre, the files naming names in the city's litiga-
tion … an optimism built in dead turkey & canola
oil & the inevitability of flow over Niagara Falls,
though Susan Howe reckons they can close it off or
are working on doing so in times of … basic
English … like Rockefeller's mates convincing him
clearing and drainage of swamps are part of a cycle
of philanthropy, & students might be driven into an
artificial lake should a riot foil the hospital architecture—the asylum tour …

Buffalo, largely because of Charles Bernstein, Susan
Howe and the stream of innovative-poet guests coming
through at all hours of the day, was the magnet for
Language. That's why I felt I had to go there. I was disappointed with poetics in Australia: theory there was the
enemy, not a tool. I'd dropped out of university late in my
second year to write, travel, take drugs, drink, wreak
havoc. I'd ended up in Cambridge. I'd get an MA there as
a Fellow, I'd earn an MA through Edith Cowan University,
I'd go on to get a PhD. You're always treated as an outsider
if you don't have the bits of paper. I despise the bits of
paper. They aren't about poetry, or art. The smartest of
poets—Robert Adamson—had little formal education. I

am an auto-didact: I have taught myself—well, and poorly. But I have always mistrusted, even loathed, the university system. (I have been planning a new school of environmental poetics, to work with and against universities. That's another story.) Yet here I was, doing the US university and college circuit. Here I was, with the poet–academics. There's no other choice: as John Forbes said to me once, 'I have spent my life reading books.' I have spent my life playing and working through theories. I did research science as a teenager. I had a laboratory. I craved ideas. The Language poets, now melded with academia, had also made their own academia; had gravitated there out of financial and intellectual need.

So, there I was. I went to a party where a student offered me a cut-out polyhedron and rhomboidal poem; a professor leered at a brilliant female student. Brilliant was the turn-on. They all drank. I remained sober. The loneliness was palpable there, the community of absence, all the overlays hiding a loneliness, I told myself as I left. I met the renowned poet Robert Creeley that night, but I think we both seemed a little nonplussed by each other. And I started to realise my poetics came from a fusion not of Language and the wheatbelt of Western Australia but of the linguistic interiorities of Cambridge and the wheatbelt. American Language poetry is about America, and nothing more.

The flight from Buffalo was one of the worst of my life. (One worse: the door blowing off the 747 I travelled in from Singapore to Bombay in 1984. It happened at 8000 feet, so we survived, though stuff went out the door and people were dragged against their seatbelts. They dumped fuel and returned to Singapore.) But out of Buffalo, a fierce lightning storm. I have been struck twice by lightning in the flesh; on that occasion the plane was struck by lightning. An entire football team—blokes bigger than their seats—wept and screamed at the back of the plane.

Bettina, my agent, wanted to meet Charles Bernstein. We were made welcome in the small but comfortable Upper West Side apartment. A young girl trying to look ten years older glanced in, and went out. Charles said she was thirteen going on thirty. I could believe it. Their son was mucking around and friendly: smart as a tack.

Charles was keen for me to look at the work of his wife, the artist Susan Bee. Like many successful men, he was overtly anxious that his wife's accomplishments be recognised. It makes it easier for them. For them both. Bettina felt uncomfortable. Charles made comments about the Holocaust. Being German, she wasn't sure how to reply, other than to make awkward apologies for her nation's past.

I feel Charles, being Jewish, had the right to speak as he did. The sheer appalling loss of it. Later, Bettina was incensed. How does he know that my family weren't part of the resistance? My family were always against the Nazis. I cannot be held accountable for the past! She was so angry and hurt that she couldn't cry. I wasn't sure what to say, although I fully understood where Charles was coming from. I say the same to all non-indigenous Australians about Australia's genocide of Aboriginals. We are all responsible for the past.

Charles. Compact. Neat. Glasses. Suit-like attire. New York drawl. Wry. Ironic. Demonstratively non-demonstrative. Wants to know why the *New Yorker* doesn't take Language poetry seriously. Why they don't try! Poetically ambitious, in his own way, he has a way of showing interest when not interested, of not showing interest when interested. Poetry business/anti-business radical. Star of the Yellow Pages television commercial. Guru. Willing and able. Conversationalist. Enthusiast. Not averse to comforts and adulation.

15

Blue velvet

URS JAEGGI really is one of the most remarkable and talented people I've met. Our collaboration on the fax book was only one manifestation of a mutual enthusiasm that spanned, really, about two or three years. We read together on a few occasions, most notably at the 'East Berlin Literaturhaus'—and in Hamburg. The Hamburg event was unusual, to say the least, and made for an extensive article (or maybe bemusement—the critic didn't know what the hell we were on about; did *we*?) in the *Tag* the following day. Urs did some radio promotion for the event but was upset with the interviewer, who merely wanted to discuss Urs's past glories as a novelist. Urs had just got back from one of his regular trips to visit his mother at their hometown in Switzerland.

Urs is an imposing man—one who seems larger than he actually is. His baldness gives him that experienced look, his round glasses the wise look, none of which he cultivates. Urs 'just is': a powerful intellectual force that enjoys the physical world but is trapped somewhere between the two. Other people were constantly telling me how attractive he is to women. He spoke a little of an earlier partner, but more of her film work than of her. I was told later that she is a pre-eminent 'woman director' in Germany. So much of him was in the clean lines of his high-ceilinged apartment. The room I slept in contained a rocking horse, which, in my couple of hours of uneasy sleep, made me think of a nightmare horse in Fuseli's painting. Urs's sketches and drawings are filed in the cabinet drawers of his studio apartment.

We walked down to Berlin's 'Zoo District', past the porn and sex shops, to a restaurant. Urs made social comments about the wealthy and how they liked to display themselves. There's an immense and intense generosity there, but also an intractable will at work. He was willing to push art as far as it could go.

Urs took me to a soirée at his Berlin agent's place, to introduce me. It was an occasion of drinking and eating where I did neither drinking nor eating. People took coats and so on off at the door, as one does in Europe; I kept mine on. I was highly strung, but it being a gathering of writers, and many of them the eminent German writers of the day, there were many highly strung among them. I hit it off with the young Austrian writer Raoul Schrott and spent much of the time chatting with him. That was Berlin.

In Hamburg, my agent, who had become 'our agent', at least temporarily, had put us up in a cylinder of glass by the docks. It was architecturally like the mountain of the Purgatorio, though comfortable and 'chic'. Bettina had style, and enjoyed style. Urs had moved over to Bettina from his previous agent, who had been unable to sell his experimental works to publishers. Bettina would meet with the same problem: 'They just want one of your regular novels ...'

It was with Urs that I spent one of the most artistically radical and genuinely experimental moments of my life—so much is not genuinely so in the world of the pseudo-avant-gardes—at an arthouse cinema in Hamburg. The night started around 9pm: texts by Urs Jaeggi and John Kinsella, film shown simultaneously—my favourite, the ur-film of ur-films, David Lynch's *Blue Velvet*. I'd written to Dennis Hopper, one of the film's stars, a year or so before, had based my novel *Genre* partly on the script of *Blue Velvet* which I watched thirteen times consecutively (until delirious) and wrote the script out from memory, and as I went, with the viewings. Urs created texts for the occasion; I basically used my poem 'Syzygy', which I cut and pasted and rearranged as I went, extrapolated, interpolated, and adjusted in response to his texts. We were both dressed in black and wearing headset radio microphones, the film was showing (I think it also had subtitles in German), and we walked through and over the audience. People, it has to be said, *were* nonplussed!

On a more subtle note, experimental also, the night I read with Charles Bernstein at the Segue Foundation in

New York made the grade: not on my part, but on that of Charles, who read a long poem punctuating each pause in the flow with a tiny bell, which he rang short and sharp: *bringgg, bringgg*. It was a moment of supreme irony and self-mockery. For whom the bell tolls.

Postscript: A few days after I got back to Cambridge, to Tracy and Katherine, I received a letter in the mail from a woman who'd attended my Hamburg events (I also did a conventional reading at the Literaturhaus or some other venue), who had decided that I might be able to guide her on the path to artistic enlightenment. She outlined a scenario in which I was the king and she the queen and our artistic epiphany would come in one great mytho-climax … I have never asked Urs if he received something similar.

16

Downriver

SOMEONE TOLD ME that the poet Sean O'Brien was walking along the banks of the Tyne in Newcastle, England,
with the poet Jo Shapcott, a copy of JH Prynne's new
Poems in hand … that he read a few of the poems (aloud,
I am guessing) and then unceremoniously threw the volume
into the river. About six months ago, Bob Ellis, the
Australian author, political speechwriter and old university
mate of Les Murray's, came up to me frothing in fury with
the story I'd told about Prynne disowning his first volume
of poems, and about how it had mysteriously disappeared
from university libraries—presumably taken by readers
either acting in the belief that they were protecting the
'master's' legacy or acting on his (publicly undeclared, one
should add) wish that it cease to exist. Ellis's fury was so

intense (saying, oddly, 'It's like the Nazis burning books') that I had to point out that Prynne had not condoned such actions and had every right to disown his own earlier work. For me, the book trade is just another way of abusing nature: of cutting down trees and calling it necessary. And here I am, right in the middle of it. These contradictions inform most things we do or say, and Sean's book dumping doesn't mean much on the face of it.

Sean O'Brien, apart from being one of the best poets writing in Britain, is one of the nation's best and most belligerent critics. Widely deplored for taking on the 'avant-garde' head-on, what he actually opposes is any form of 'school'. He distrusts what he sees as the Cambridge mafia, despite the fact that he went to Cambridge himself. He sees in Prynne the legions of enslaved imitators of whom Prynne himself is sceptical. O'Brien and Prynne have more in common than one might think. O'Brien perhaps might say that our own interaction has led to a small (very small) belief that different 'camps' can share interests, but then again he just as soon might look to my outsider–insider status and 'over-enthusiasms'. A friend recently begrudgingly admired 'O'Brien'—'the old Rottweiler himself' was the exact expression. Enemy of experimentalism and the Cambridge poets, enemy of the avant-garde. Well, I think 'avant-garde' is a reactionary term and its militarism says it all. Sean is one of the most innovative poets writing, with a mind the size of Cambridge (or bigger), who has a public politics to boot. That's what the left is afraid of: the old left in Sean. And it seems to have credentials they might not have.

For a number of years I published with Bloodaxe Books; it was because of the way the editor there, Neil Astley, targeted Sean that I left them. Astley claims I went elsewhere because he rejected a manuscript of mine (*TV*, which he said indulged all my bad experimental traits and none of my absorbable 'landscape' traits), but it was actually more to do with what I saw as a double standard of condemning prize culture and awards while playing up to them and manipulating them to a degree unseen before in Britain, unless it be through Faber's historic TS Eliot-driven monopoly on high literary cultures (in the twentieth century). Astley accused O'Brien of favouring certain poets when judging a competition, and actually made the accusation public. There is no impartiality in judging books. Astley knows this better than anyone.

So, reacting to what I felt was a hypocritical attack on Sean, I made it clear I wanted to leave Bloodaxe, good as I consider them as a press. The picture is made more complex because at that stage Gerry Wardle, Sean's wife, was my agent. Rather than encourage me in my action, she strongly discouraged it: it was bad business to leave Bloodaxe. In other words, it was a tangled relationship in every sense of the word. But that's what poetry friendships and publishing are.

I think I first met Sean and Gerry together at a reading near Newcastle—inseparable couple that they are (I've always liked inseparable couples—makes me feel secure, even if as an illusion … it's something I respect, loyalty). It's where I had my first experience of Sean the flexible rather than rigid and unforgiving critic he'd been painted. Sean had reviewed my book *The Undertow: Selected Poems* in the *TLS*. It was a partly favourable and partly condemning review. He was sceptical about my very experimental work 'Syzygy', which he found redundant and not as innovative as I thought it was. I read (or performed!) an extract from 'Syzygy' that night. Sean said: 'I hadn't realised it was so funny, so ironic ...' He turned and repeated it to Gerry who replied, 'Well, Sean, you wrote what you thought at the time ...' Which was fine by me.

Sean—portly, as they say, clutching a satchel of books and papers to his side, smelling of whiskey, rubbing a middling beard with his other hand, occasionally wiping perspiration from his brow into his salt-and-pepper (more pepper than salt) hair, or pushing his hand under his glasses, lifting them as he rubbed sweat from around his nose and eyes—spoke to me through Gerry. Sharon Olds had done something similar. Gerry spoke fast where Sean lilted and almost panted his words slowly, growlingly out. She tripped over her words and stuttered a little but gave the impression of sharpness and organisation. They counterpointed each other: Gerry was thin, neat and precise; Sean, large, generous in his word usage and honed to kill. I liked them a great deal. They thought, I am sure, that I was manic, out of control and probably a little mad. Eventually Sean and I read together at the Dublin Poetry Festival with the World Cup on and the Irish team playing for their lives. Sean cut his reading short and moved off to the nearest radio. A poet with priorities other than himself. I liked it! Walking back to the hotel, I was abused by drunken football fans, furious that their team had lost.

17

Oprah, Tracy, and George, and Tracy

AS I WRITE I have been following the drama between Oprah Winfrey and the author James Frey over his 'memoir' *A Million Little Pieces*, his recounting of a life of drugs and alcohol and extreme behaviour, the fastest seller (2 million copies plus) on Oprah's Book Club (what a joke)—the defence and then indignation that he had fabricated details of this memoir, 'fictionalised' to make a better story. Edward Wyatt in the *New York Times* (January 27) writes:

> 'I made a mistake,' Mr. Frey (pronounced fry) replied, adding that he had developed a tough-guy image of himself as a 'coping mechanism' to help address his alcohol and drug addiction. 'And when I

was writing the book,' he said, 'instead of being as introspective as I should have been, I clung to that image.'

It was a stunning bit of drama that had people throughout the publishing industry glued to their television sets yesterday afternoon.

It's stuff to play with. Stuff to revel over. I ask: what does anyone expect of the alcoholic and/or drug addict? Truth? Selling two million copies was a good deal. A dry drunk, maybe. Truth is dangerous, not life-enhancing. When I say that my memory is hazy, it can be selectively so, or genuinely stuffed up from damaging the brain itself. Frey had clearly been there, but truth has to be *real* (commonly held) truth, when it never is for a drunk or an addict. So, he didn't have his root canals done without anaesthetic?

'Deceiver!' they say, wheeling out addicts who'd been in the same rehab clinic and known of others needing dental treatment. Well, I had a molar taken out without anaesthetic because I'd just come off shit. I haven't taken drugs or alcohol since 1995, and yet, in reality, I remain in the 'recovery' mode. Only a fool thinks he has escaped addiction. Escaped it and engaged with *real* truth. I don't think I know what that is ...

The Oprahs of the world (with their life of addictions—from food to hype) require truth, they require the 'redemption', to make sense of the decay and collapse around them. It's all based on guilt and bliss woven together. The book club member addicted to pharmaceuticals or the extra-strong coffee in the morning to get going, the strung-out Weight Watchers client needing to know that extremity is classifiable and escapable from. If you make money without it being 'illegal', you've succeeded.

Tracy used to remark, when people quizzed her over how she'd got involved with a junkie: 'He could seem so together, so cogent, and he was highly successful at what he did: not what you're led to believe a junkie would be like'. Of course, living with me, she saw the extremes—especially the drama of scoring—and quickly revised her opinion.

I know that I shouldn't include my partner—my wife—in a book like this. But why not, really? And what the hell is a book like this? I started writing it because, frankly, I needed the dough. Then I didn't want to write it, because talking about the living and the recently dead in such a personal way is particularly difficult. Then I decided I was writing it to understand how a 'literary life' unfolds. I think it's a work about making sense of a world I distrust and often dislike but feel compelled to be part of. The people described here have been friends and peers and have loved (and hated) poetry, which can consume everything around you. So this is really a book about obsessions, if not about poems themselves. It's about all that goes on around writing poems: the paraphernalia of a writing life. Given that, how can any of it make sense for me without Tracy being in there? She also shadows this book in other ways. Because there is much I cannot say, and because she has been reading family memoirs (of *her* family), she has a desire to record things as she's seen them, to say the things I cannot say in this book. Not to publish, but to archive. She has been writing a shadow memoir. I have not read it, and she probably won't let me read it (she usually doesn't). So, she's entangled in this in so many ways, though she has no direct role in my memories, no role in the drafting and no role in what the book means or says. But she's there.

Professor George Steiner, doyen of comparative literature, has always been kind and harsh with me at once. He is one reason Cambridge has been so important to me. Churchill College and George are inseparable. We all (Tracy, Katherine and myself) went to his and his wife Zara's place in Cambridge for lunch one day. Zara showed us where George's office would be in the garden, now that he'd retired. George was agitated and wanted to talk about a manuscript of my poems he had, which he'd later 'blurb'—*The Hunt*. He praised and condemned at once. He told me to ward off the vignettes, to concentrate on the narrative. He said there was a difference between verse and poetry, that he'd written verse and that the one book of it was in the Churchill Library—that was it, and should be it. He talked about form and purpose. George believes in the moral efficacy of the poem: in the message in conjunction with (and out of) 'language'. I started writing a series of 'ethical poems' in response to this (and other) discussions, about what made a poem necessary: they have never been collected, and maybe they can never be completed. I did publish one about an injured pigeon (found on the College green) in the poetry collection *Zoo*.

So, George was quite critical but also supportive. I took the criticisms on board and reworked the book—to its betterment, I think. He has such a harsh reputation (I have literally

seen eminent academics who are George's friends quiver
with the memory of being dressed down by him; he did it
to me once, and it was brutal, over an invitation I extended
to him which he felt it was not my right to extend) that it
amazed me he could be so pastoral and even parental when
it came to our family unit. Zara and George had lived earlier in the Sheppard Flats—where we lived for four years in
Cambridge—and knew the building's shortcomings. In
fact, they were the first to live in these now heritage-pro-
tected block-architecture modernist buildings (when John
Forbes visited us, the first thing he remarked on was how
he'd studied the architecture of these flats at university,
especially that of the chapel). Zara commented on the lim-
itations of the flats' kitchens, of raising children there, of
the improvements she and George had suggested.

They fussed over us. They were warm to us. But then
George could say something biting, as he did on an occasion when talking with Tracy (I wasn't there): that children
should not be entirely protected from frightening things—
images or talk of violence, for example, on television. In a
Paris Review interview of 1995, George describes how as
a child of five in Paris he was encouraged by his father to
look out the window at marchers who were shouting,
'Death to the Jews!'. His father said, 'You must never be
frightened; what you're looking at is called history.' In the
interview George comments, 'I think that sentence may
have formed my whole life.'

George was a child of the Holocaust, and one cannot
underestimate the pain and damage he has lived with his

whole life. He mastered English (and other languages) at a young age. He was born in Paris in 1929, and was taken from there to America in 1940, with the invasion of France by the Germans. George told us that his father had insisted on his learning English, because English was a language of America, the 'land of the future'. That it would all be about America. As a Jewish émigré, he was gripped and haunted by the death camps, though away from them. The horror has almost impelled him in his search to find humanity in people, and especially in literature and language, where it seems to be absent, or vanquished.

There is much of Paul Célan (1920–1970), the most essential post-Second World War poet writing in German, in Steiner—in the man. I wouldn't say it's in his critical language, but it's in his conceptualisations. Steiner himself has called Célan 'almost certainly the major European poet in the period after 1945'. Losing his family to the Holocaust, living in permanent exile from Romania, Célan wrote his poems of language-loss in German (the language of his mother) as a confrontation with the brutalities carried out in its name, in its substance. He wrote poems in fragments, remnants, residues—all that was left to him after the atrocities, after his witnessing and experiencing (in a labour camp). In his most famous poem, 'Todesfuge', he wrote 'Death is a master from Deutschland'.

Many have also commented on the absolute bleakness of George's view of the world: the destruction of language and culture through totalitarianism and extremism. But knowing George the person a little (a very little, really), I have always felt he has written that way wishing it were not so. If you hear him speak proudly of his daughter's academic successes, or his wife's, or of a rollicking occasion with the dubious poet of the ex-Soviet Union Yevgeny Yevtushenko at the Steiner house in Cambridge (large, free-standing, on the edge of the town, full of books with calming garden views from the windows ... there are some great photos of Zara framed by these windows on the net ... white hair like a halo of serenity ... but nothing is that easy, and she was formed in the belief that genius is difficult to live with ...) after too much drink, his joy in gossip, his amusement at an error, his indignation at being treated poorly, which we all share, his joy at having his achievements recognised, and his 'red rag to a bull' whispering, 'but without political oppression where is the great art?', you realise that the breadth of his critical mind comes out of the conflicts of his personality.

This does not prevent George taking a figure like the German philosopher Martin Heidegger and tackling him head-on, contextually and specifically. In many ways, father of comparative literature, he has moved across languages and cultures with respect, often finding humanity in what many would consider 'evil'. Célan's understandable (essential) choices are not necessarily Steiner's own, but they share a common ground and necessity.

In a room of people, George Steiner is never silent. He expects people to come to him, and they do. He is a showman as well; his famous lecturing flamboyance rubs off on the listener, and one literally feels part of his circle (when he wants you to: he can turn on you suddenly, and vehemently).

I don't mind the extremes: as the cliché goes, it's part of his brilliance. When he talks with you about your work, he does so closely (leaning towards you conspiratorially and indulgently, he can 'pah' you and lean back, he can give an impish smile … he is a gossip, a raconteur, a case for anger management, and calmness itself). He is illuminated.

It is worth noting that among staff at Heffers Bookshop—a Cambridge icon—George was considered to be the complete gentleman. He was always warm and polite, and never condescending to booksellers.

Most times I see George, he warns me about my fascination for 'Prynne'. It's a dangerous cult, he says—students losing their minds to the incomprehensible. The ineffable, I might answer. He has you too, might be the reply. But he loves it: George loves the 'cult of Prynne'.

George has a wonder for science, and he often praises the great scientists who have been through Churchill College. In this praise, ironically, he creates a separation of the two cultures, creates a space for 'great literature' where Derrida and others cross-pollinate and maybe weaken the text. It's not my position, and maybe it's not his, but you get a sense of it in conversation. He marvels that in Newton's time a scientist or thinker could know 'everything', but not now by a long, long way. The world of computers has not left him behind, but made him resolute, if marvelling. If you get a note from George, it is on a small slip of paper and typed on a manual typewriter.

I once discussed the Nobel Prize with him, and he rejected his 'eligibility', saying that he could only take such a thing if Derrida (and one other) got it at the same time. On the way home from that lunch with the Steiners, Zara said to us, 'I hope you didn't get too offended by what George said', meaning his comments on my manuscript. I assured her that it was welcome, that I appreciated it. She mentioned how many friends had turned their backs on them because of George's bluntness. Zara—an eminent historian and long-time Fellow of New Hall, Cambridge—is a compact, generous and warm woman who, like Jeanne Bloom, seems essential to her partner's equilibrium. As I've said, I admire such relationships, always aware that they must have their own difficulties. George was extremely proud of Zara's forthcoming book, *The Lights that Failed: European International History 1919–1933*.

I remember George's glee when Ted Hughes's *Tales from Ovid* came out. The controversy over whether it was translation or not seemed to delight him: I love it, he said. George emphatically believes that reading itself is an act of translation, as he makes clear in his book *After Babel* (1975). He also loved it because Hughes was published by his own publisher, Faber & Faber. George likes to be part of the best. It's like writing for the *TLS*. There's a hierarchy of culture, of criticism, and these are the preservers of a destroyed (and 'deconstructed', real or imagined) artistic aspiration.

Often my guests coming to High Table at Churchill would time their visits to coincide with George dining. When my play *Crop Circles* was put on in Churchill, George was generous yet restrained. He wrote, with affection and irony: 'Thornton Wilder would have approved! As did, within the limits of poor hearing,—my fault? the actors'?—your most obdt. and faithful servant, George.'

I find myself thinking about George through Tracy ... But it was Tracy herself as poet, publishing in the late 1980s, that really attracted my interest. The first issue of *Salt* carried a batch of her poems. That was 1990, and I'd heard a lot about her from Anthony Lawrence and others. I was interested, at that stage, as fellow poet. My then partner took a dislike to Tracy when we visited her and her daughter at the Katharine Susannah Prichard Centre in about 1991. I don't know why: intuition, maybe, about my interest in her work (and that's what it was then).

Tracy and I can't quite remember when we first met. She remembers well when she first saw me: at a reading when I 'nodded off' on the stage. We saw each other on a train in about 1990, and I said hello. She later said she'd wondered if I was the poet, but wasn't sure until just before I got off at Kelmscott station. The Perth 'poetry scene' was small, inward-looking, and volatile. I was anti-social in my addictive behaviour; she was not a social animal. We met, despite the odds.

Epilogue:
the wheatbelt diaries

Katherine is still in hospital. Just back from the bookshop—10.15pm. Tracy drove me down. I need to start a new journal to keep my sanity. This is a grim time. I need to write—take notes. Not a lot is happening on paper and the poems/lines are churned into one conglomeration in my head at the moment. Have ideas, but they won't come out in the way I'd like them to. So, this book. Maybe … I'm thinking of Olson's 'Small birds, to age with the leaves, come in the Fall'.

25th May, 2001

Just cancelled the Kenyon Summer School workshop, the Ledbury Festival, and BBC Fine Lines recording with Craig Raine. Katherine's health must come first—we need to return to Australia asap. A tough night—carnage and substance nightmares. But in my waking state I'm steady. The insecurities of sleep are not going to unsettle me. I search through the window for the pileated woodpecker, the white-tailed deer, the woodchuck, the crows.

5th/6th June, 2001
York! Western Australia (arrive June 4th)

Town. Racism in rural Australia. The Trial (sun, scandal). GM lupins escape.

11th June, 2001

[titles for 3 poems]
1. Roof Lost in a High Wind

2. The Burning of the Hay Stack

'Laved in flame as in sacrament ...' (Thomas Merton—'Elegy for the Monastery Barn')

3. Truck Overturned in Fog

On Racism and Religious Bigotry in the WA Wheatbelt:
e.g. On the Brethren in Dalwallinu, Dowerin ... by the non-Brethren farmers' (Anglo-Celts!) kids:

'Own it all.'

'Wives scrawny pasty-faced stick insects with scarves. Look smug!'

'Odd.'

'Steal trucks from wheat bins.'

'People speak in hushed voices.'

'Everybody else leaves town.'

'Standover merchants.'

'Steal trucks from the silos and threaten to put people out of business.'

'One-way ticket.'

'No music, newspapers or radios!'

'Not short of money ...'

'Big expensive cars.'

The wheatbelt is the bastion of Anglo-Celts resisting 'the foreigners'. They are also strongly anti-boat-people, anti-Asian, etc. Racism is endemic. Homophobia is rife.

19th June, 2001

A warm winter! 22 degrees Celsius today after a cold night. The mountain lifted out of the fog this morning. The hill of tears, as it is known by its people. It calls to them.

20th June, 2001

Out at Wheatlands—in the corner of the main block—which was inherited by Uncle Gerry and

Auntie Lorraine from Auntie Elsie. Most of it is under crop—or struggling to come into crop given the unseasonal dry. Leased by Ken.

The jiddy jiddy (willy wagtail) has the biggest personality in the bush …

The bark, drying from the fog, cracks—tree vibrates with heat exchange. A pair of budgies feeding between furrows. Perching on adjacent fenceposts, balancing on rusted strands of barbed wire over the salt run-off. The polluted well—Dynamic Lifter. Talon—rodenticide! 'Bury all rodent bodies …'

Evening.

Preparation of the garden. Trench digging. Straw mulch. Yellow and white sand to thin out the heavy red soil. Breaking up the clay. Watering by timer.

12th July, 2001

I have a 'harrowing' poem in mind … in reaction to working on the Dransfield book and thinking about the set of harrows sitting on Auntie Elsie's old block (corner of Taylor and Station roads). They edge salt and fertile ground. They covered the seed of the crop, which hung in despite the chronically late rains!—but also edge the torn-open ground of the salt—from where the prophets come (Brady—a *real* saint)—that harrowed releases them unrecognised—to be harrowed again in the hopes that the order of 'patriarchs and prophets'—their souls—might make another go of it. Seize the moment.

Also in mind, Katherine's terrible situation … Her illness IS my poetry at the moment. It saddens me so much—I love her dearly.

10th September, 2001

The cold/wet has come now. But a dry winter—barely enough to stimulate the crops—though late rains will mean a drive towards full 'seed' growth. Already have a semi-impoverished harvest poem in mind. The last week has been difficult.

… This the nature of the (Western) Australian 'character'?—suspicious and vengeful, full of frustration and an almost superstitious ignorance come out of 'neglect' and 'isolation'?

Yenyenning poems. Angles of seeing from County Peak. Personality is a variable and not a constant.

26th October, 2001

Back from London/Cambridge on 24th. Very jet-lagged. An idea for a new volume of poems—*Swoon*. I, the male, swoon …

The warmth—I love the warmth. It is seedtime (not seeding time) in York. The grass is high with late rains and the bees are thick in the Paterson's Curse.

19th July, 2002

3 in the morning.

Those bastards our neighbours doing their firebreaks with Roundup.

Evening. Watching the bats between the mountain and York gums, shed, house and moon. Long radical flights. Conflicting, then in tune with each other, following 'erratic' flight paths of insects.

20th July, 2002

Colder today. Striated light. One doesn't 'milk' a subject, one becomes possessed by it. One angle tells little—and the light is always changing.

Burning off on the way back from Wallaby Hills nature reserve—is it the fire that clarifies the evening or the evening that clarifies the fire? We will visit the reserve regularly over the next couple of months and note the changes—emergences of orchids etc. Always the Needlings as an 'aside', then Mount Bakewell as focus. The drama of vista.

23rd July, 2002

Old corner block of Wheatlands. Auntie Elsie's. Hay lifter still here. Dam still dryish and engorged with corrugated iron and wire. Well still choked and bitter with poison. But furrows of tea-tree plantings. She-oaks. 28 parrots, willy wagtails, honey-eaters. Thin still water with attendant scum on salt flats—reflecting clear blue winter sky. Sown fields green but low. Old wet-cell car battery molten and torn open at positive end. Zinc cells decomposing and plastic brittle. An ecology of weeds, ants, other insects built around it. Filaments of light-reaching growth beneath battery impression/light-deprivation suggests generations of seeds wreathed by worms, centipedes, ants sheltering. Still holding water.

Low-flying red birds, salt bush hoverers, all quickly moving—deleted by constant drone of small plane.

18th August, 2002

Warm clear day—brilliant! The fact that I pissed a bucket of blood yesterday doesn't seem to matter. I am hoping to get permission to climb Bakewell/ Walwalinj with Stephen this afternoon.

Sitting in the mid-morning sunlight under the straggly branches of a York gum. It's late winter so the bark is stripping away—hanging in ribbons, in metallic curls and coils. Looking up through the canopy, the leaves glisten like stainless steel scales. Technology mirrors the natural world, though it struggles to make something 'new' by removing it to the power of, to the next place.

It is wonderful to see how happy Katherine is here. Even when she has difficult spells she manages to overcome them by connecting with the 'outside'—there's space and birds and a world of adventure. She has mapped the place as 'Kate Town'.

Tracy is resting this morning—a difficult night. It is awkward for her not to be able to sleep on her stomach. We are very excited about the pregnancy.

A white-faced heron has just landed in the upper-most branch of a gum. It loped into the tree—guttural croak, huge wings and snaking neck negotiating the branches, leaf-clusters.

Sir Philip Sidney:

> Feed on my sheep; my charge, my comfort, feed;
> With sun's approach your pasture fertile grows,
> O only sun that such fruit can breed.

Surrounded by flycatchers and weebills! They dart between a lone York gum, pasture weeds in between, and the stand of York gums along the uncleared roadway (just fences and bush). The red-capped robin proves to be two—a pair of males. Making the same movements—chirruping like the staccato of a twig on tightened paper. Excited and frenetic with the sunlight and strata of insects flying over the pasture.

A female robin is around as well!

Stephen and I just ushered a yellow-rumped thornbill out of the shadehouse. It was exhausted but clearly relieved to have escaped!

24th August, 2002

Saturday. Nice just to chat and cuddle Tracy in bed this morning—haven't had much of a chance to do this over the last few weeks. Have been extremely busy, and the medical stuff has been disturbing ... So it goes.

The Brockman lecture went well. It's nice to hear people saying that they agree that she's a major poet. I sit now under the 'purple mountain', with acacias surrounding me as I write this. It's something we share. I will drive out to Seabrook today. That familiar drone of small planes—parachute drops. It is a brilliant spring-like day. Grasshoppers have started to appear and the pasture is alive with them. I am routinely angry with the people on the neighbouring property who sprayed their firebreaks a couple of days ago. Haven't seen many birds this morning, but it's a refuge situation—their song is everywhere. The bright sun, the early morning—all keep them hidden in the foliage of York gums and acacias. Just before dawn, even without my glasses, I could sense the purple light haloing Bakewell/Walwalinj ... A white-faced heron just landed nearby. That plane droning again—might also be a crop-duster working the other side of the mountain. Argghhh! A wattle bird just arced by. And I can hear the golden-whistler jetting air into a graceful harmonic. An electric syrinx.

Stephen was telling me that the guy that bought H-block is a gun nut. A few months after buying the place he lost a limb geligniting a fox den. The road at the end of his block carries a road sign with three foxes impaled on it.

1st September, 2002

First day of Spring. York, Western Australia.

Cold fronts are rushing over. Gale force gusts. Under the red-capped robin tree. Three mils in the rain-gauge overnight. A week since the death of Dorothy [Hewett] and the white-faced herons are nowhere to be seen. They say a crow interrupted Kate Lilley's reading of a poem at Dorothy's funeral—a visitation. But she's not with the crows, she's with the white-faced herons. Atheists are always the strongest believers!

Took J. [Jeremy Prynne] to Toodyay today ... We visited an op shop and a needlecraft shop where he bought a kaleidoscope for Katherine.

Took J. to King's Park [in Perth] and we discussed the need for Australia to become a republic. There's more empire in Australia than in Britain!

The mountain is oscillating between the afternoon's heavy and light cloud. Sun appears in patches and electrifies the white trunks of the redwood and wandoo on the upper outcrops. They easily become figures. They are certainly of the Dreaming. The rain is holding off but will come again soon. I write against its arrival, though wish for it. The ground is still dry a few inches down.

Tracy is inside working on a translation of *Godot*, I think—Katherine is still sleeping. There is a temporary calm in the house. Wild radishes and Paterson's Curse are in flower and being twirled by the wind. Small birds are cutting sharp manoeuvres to thwart the winds. They can be heard despite the vast swell, the deluge in the trees. The sun is coming through as Morse code.

My body has been sick with the stress of Dorothy's death, and my mind trapped. Giving a lecture on her work was cathartic, up to a point. Poetry is the only way out of the maze.

J. carries a small magnifying glass and likes to examine things 'close up'. It's the evocation and the mapping of the micro that rebuilds as lyrical sound patterns—as resonances. The surfaces are gestures, polished away. Chipped at, then polished away. They remain as echoes.

Wind is picking up. Very strong gusts—watching a butterfly being flicked about, trying to find a flight path. It is a dark blur now up near the canopy.

12th June, 2003

Arrival back in York from Ohio on 9th. An eventful and tiring journey—five month old bub as well as K. Diverted because of a massive volcanic eruption—ash in the upper atmosphere. Had to take on fuel in Fiji …

18th June, 2003

Gwambygine Pools. A place of the Wagyl …

Laterite soils. 1000 kilos of salt per hectare. The signs. 1500 kg of salt a minute when the Avon is glowing full-throttle. Salt built up over millennia via rain lifted from the oceans. They 'trained' the river and destroyed it. The pools of Gwambygine are one of the few places where they didn't 'train' the deep pools (only place of water during summer). Long-necked tortoises and sacred kingfishers here. So thinned out, denuded. In 1938 the white parents of children at Gwambygine School voted to remove Aboriginal students. Earlier, the school had stipulated a 'similar level of hygiene' as the white kids. The signs. The signs say even that wasn't good enough. The signs. The whites brought a violence to everything in their new place. They conflated land and plants and animals and the people who were here before them.

24th June, 2003

Heavy fog this morning. Outline of mountain faintly visible—though maybe this is expectation rather than visual certainty. On the high ground in front of the house the York gums twist up through the cushioning.

Wallaby Hills:
Deep into the reserve. Patchy rain cloud. Humid but not warm. Bad cold. Feverish—flies pinpoint. Stands of mallee, wandoo, redwood, even swamp melaleuca on watershed of sand to gravel. Higher up, banksias and she-oak stands. Hakeas intense! Insane with echidna diggings in bark-strewn bases of wandoos where termites are beginning their work. Fallen wandoos eaten out. An echidna hollow under one. Fresh occupation. Despite it being winter, a sluggish blue-tongue goanna sunning itself in the intermittencies of cloud/sun/cloud. Still, an ultra-violent dense sunlight. Wind ravaging the canopy. Termite mounds abound. All falls to the ravine.

Gullies slicing into the ravine. Quartz outcrops. Chalky stone. Saltbush and samphire. Sparse stands of melaleuca. Threatening and welcoming, brooding and consuming. It possesses you. The kind of atmosphere that was exploited in *Picnic at Hanging Rock*—the film version. Prescience. In the surrounding district, late crops are going in. Some are being resown. Dogs running ahead of John Deere and Case tractors dragging seeders through the ploughed red loam. Kangaroo droppings.

The wind hides the birds—but they are there. The parrots and weebills, wattlers and flycatchers.

The sun, on its rollercoaster of cloud, stills then churns the blood of the place. It has no bodily equivalent, though it agitates your body.

Uphill. Ironstone gravel. Vegetation changes. Flies thick—fuming. Forget the names we give—concentrate on the angle, shape, light, touch and sound.

It's the beginning of 2006 and the family is living back at York, in the Western Australian wheatbelt. It's been a weird summer—record January rainfall, storms ... as I look out across paddocks that should be red-brown dirt and sun-bleached stubble, they are green-yellow and thick with wild radish. The seasons *are* altering and, sadly, I am part of that ... I am about to leave for Cambridge where I don't doubt things will be climatically unusual as well. Later this year I'll head back to the United States, where in our last winter in Ohio we were without power or heating for five days as the result of a severe ice storm, in sub-freezing temperatures. This hit around the same time as the Indian Ocean tsunami, which made us feel as if we had little to complain about.

Crows are squabbling in the York gums, and their sharp-then-drawn-out caws cut across the songs of the honeyeaters and thornbills singing close to the house. Actually, thinking about it, it sounds like a mixture of Little Crows and Australian Ravens cross-talking. I like to be as precise as possible.

ACKNOWLEDGEMENTS

An earlier version of a section of 'Fellow Travellers' previously appeared in *Landfall* (NZ); and an early version of 'Shock and Awe' in *Ars Interpres* (Sweden).

Thanks to Elisa Berg and the MUP editorial team; the University of Western Australia; Churchill College, Cambridge; and my partner Tracy Ryan. Also thanks to Frieda Hughes.

Thanks to the following for permission to reproduce quoted material: pages 16–18: 'The Ghost of John Forbes' by Dorothy Hewett, reproduced with permission from Fremantle Arts Centre Press; page 29: Dorothy Hewett quote from *Wheatlands* by Dorothy Hewett and John Kinsella, reproduced with permission from Fremantle Arts Centre Press; page 29: extract from 'Legend of the Green Country' by Dorothy Hewett, reproduced with permission from Fremantle Arts Centre Press; page 101: extract from '3 Songs for Charles Darwin' by John Forbes, reproduced with permission from Brandl & Schlesinger; pages 103–104: 'Anti-Romantic' by John Forbes, reproduced with permission from Brandl & Schlesinger; page 105: extract from 'Ode to Karl Marx' by John Forbes, reproduced with permission from Brandl & Schlesinger; page 106: extract from 'Sydney' by John Forbes, reproduced with permission from Brandl & Schlesinger; page 128: extract from *Acrylic Tips* by JH Prynne, reproduced with permission from JH Prynne; pages 172–3: email by Amanda Ooms, reproduced with permission from Amanda Ooms; pages 181–3: extracts from 'Deconstructing Jacques Derrida' by Mitchell Stephens, reproduced with permission from Mitchell Stephens; pages 190–2: emailed letter-poem by Frieda Hughes, reproduced with permission from Frieda Hughes.